WAYS OF AQUITAINE

St.-Savin-sur-Gartempe. Nave

Ways of Aquitaine

by

FREDA WHITE

FABER AND FABER
24 Russell Square
London

First published in mcmlxviii
by Faber and Faber Limited
24 Russell Square London WC1
Printed in Great Britain by
Latimer Trend & Co Ltd Plymouth
All rights reserved

I dedicate this book to scholars. To study under the learned, to read them or listen to them is a pure and strong pleasure that I have enjoyed my life long. If I have learned nothing else, I have learned to be grateful to them. Many have been professors, who work hard and long to gain no material reward but the power of sharing their wisdom. To me they are typified by Maurice Fanshawe, who was not a professor, but a member of the information staff of the League of Nations Union, beside whom I sat at a trestle table for many years, till I knew him well, profound scholar, selfless colleague, beloved friend. Once I wrote a series of imaginary epitaphs on the staff, and the one I made for him may stand for what I feel.

> *He woke in Paradise at dawn,*
> *A bookroom opening on a lawn,*
> *And read upon the lintel-stone*
> *Nor knew the legend for his own,*
> > *'Here studies in the Eternal Schools*
> > *A sage who gladly suffered fools.'*

CONTENTS

7

Contents

Contents

MAPS

9

ILLUSTRATIONS

Illustrations

Chapter One

AQUITAINE

1. THE COUNTRY

Aquitaine is the Land of Waters. The name was given to it by the Romans, when they moved north from their colony of Narbonne in the century before Christ, and conquered almost the whole of Gaul. Aquitaine covered the great regions of central and western France, stretching north and south from the Loire to the Garonne, and east and west from the Rhone ridges of the Massif Central to the Atlantic. Later, the Roman rulers divided Aquitaine into two provinces, Aquitania Prima with Bourges as its capital, and Aquitania Secunda governed from Bordeaux. Both of these form the region of this book.

The French are great name-givers. The title of Aquitaine lasted officially for more than a thousand years, and lingers yet in a limited area east of Bordeaux, under the local form of Guienne. But most of the place-names are older than the Roman period, for they recall the Celtic tribes which the Romans found when they came. The Gauls were divided into clans under the chieftainship of princes, who usually lived in the town where the market met and the elders held council. Bourges, for instance, was the town of the Bituriges, Poitiers of the Pictaves, Saintes of the Santones. As was natural, each town was built upon a river, and the villages and farms were thickest in the river-valleys.

The traveller may look at a town or village, large or small, dominated by a cathedral of the Middle Ages or by a modern factory. Almost always it occupies the ground and bears the name

13

it has owned for as long as written history runs. Looking again, the traveller will observe that its reason for being is a river or a spring.

After the end of the Roman Empire, Aquitaine remained for centuries one of the principal parts of a France that had been torn between barbarian invaders. It was carved this way and that between rival rulers, but preserved its entity, on the whole, through the changes. This was because it was the custom of a victor to annex a whole district, capital town, people, and all, so that the tribes continued to hang together. In the later Middle Ages people were still bound by geography and racial inheritance; they might pass by war, purchase, or marriage from the lordship of one seigneur to that of another, but they still called themselves Limousin, Poitevin, Berrichon, and do so to this day.

The Revolution made changes, of course. The new governments wanted to wipe out the memory of the old feudal overlordships. They ordained new administrative boundaries, usually representing the courses of the rivers after which they are named. Thus Poitou became Vienne; Berri, Cher; Saintonge, Charente. This was logical, but as every woman knows, logic in life is not reasonable. The modern *départements* are often convenient neither for economics nor for administration. None the less, the traveller must use their names when he posts a letter, or reserves a room in an hotel. He will speak of Haute-Vienne in the Town Hall of Limoges, and of Limousin to a man whom he meets on the road.

Here I must make a confession. When I began to explore a country through which I had often driven too fast to observe it, I sought for a descriptive name for this book. I chose Aquitaine because that is an elastic term referring to a varied land. It includes regions widely contrasted. At times it has been enlarged far beyond the Roman boundaries; in the Carolingian period it was a kingdom, and stretched from the Atlantic to the borders of Provence. At other times it has shrunk to a small portion of the Roman provinces. This is an agreeable thing for a writer, for she can select what seems to her, and may seem to other travellers, places that are beautiful or interesting.

Some readers may wonder why I do not describe the Loire

itself since I propose to write about its southern tributaries. The reason is that scores of books on the Loire have appeared, some of them excellent, both in French and in English. The real reason is, I fear, due to a despicable vanity and a decent shame. The vanity consists in a wish to be among the first to write about a country; to share, in a minuscule way, in the joy of the explorer. The modesty is rooted in the fact that each time that one notices something interesting, but which others have noticed and described before, one is afraid to record it for fear that the reader may say, 'But she copied that from Jean Duplessis.' The plagiarism may be quite unconscious, and indeed I try to quote my references, when I know them; but in a region so well-trodden as the banks of the Loire, it is certain that one must be repeating the experience of others. This makes it, for me, impossible to retell a tale so often told.

2. EARTH AND WATER

Raoul Blanchard, Professor of Geology, surveyed his October intake of students in a lecture-hall of Grenoble University. He fixed and pierced us with his eye like a kestrel hovering over a thicket of finches. 'Show me the rock of which a country is made,' said he, 'and I will tell you its history.' One whose study was history and her passion mountaineering, settled to listen with rapt attention. 'At last!' she thought. 'At last a man who will tell us not only the things that happened, but why they happened.' Professor Blanchard, in that dingy hall, so long ago, was only one—though among the greatest—of the exponents of history and geology combined into what the French call 'regional geography'. I believe that nobody who attended his lectures would ever think again of human history apart from the rock, the soil, the water from which life draws its being.

Aquitaine, naturally, has suffered the enormous changes of western Europe. If you look at a contour map of France—still better, at a geological map—it is clear that it is roughly a square of land, bounded on three sides by the sea; really a promontory of Europe, connected by the Pyrenees with the further peninsula

of Spain. France itself surrounds an irregular mountain mass, the
Massif Central. The heart of that mass, and its highest hills, are
made of granite and other 'hard' rock. All around it is a selvage
of lesser, limestone hills. Then the plains stretch to the sea.

In the oldest era known to geology the sea covered most of
France. High mountains rose in a crescent centred in the Auvergne, with an eastern horn curving to the Vosges, and a western to
Brittany. Later even those were submerged under the sea for
millions of years, till the 'secondary era', some two hundred
million years ago. Then the old mountains, worn flat by the tides,
rose from the Basin of Paris to the north and the Basin of Aquitaine to the south, connected by the Strait of Poitou. It was the
Great Foldings of fifty million years ago that gave the land we see
today. Then violent eruptions lifted the Pyrenees and the Alps.
They exerted such a pressure on the Massif Central that all its
edges on the south and east were forced up in precipices and steeps.
The northern and western sides were crumpled into hundreds of
folds. The Auvergne boiled within and burst up in scores of
volcanoes. The high granitic mountains were shattered; their
present peaks are the edges of volcanic craters. The surrounding
sheath of limestone and chalk was cracked into gorges. When the
earth cooled, down the stony glens of the mountains, through the
deep gorges, the rivers flowed to the seas.

Aquitaine is itself bounded on the north by the valley of the
Loire, on the south by the Garonne. Between the two, the Massif
Central thrusts out a broad shoulder westwards, the Limousin,
nearly to the Atlantic. Its western end is joined to the ancient
hills of Brittany south of the Loire—the Vendée—by a belt of
limestone plains. This, which is a vast upland, is called along its
southern edge the Seuil de Poitou—the rim or edge of Poitou. It
never attains to more than a few hundred feet, and coming from
the Loire Valley its rise is almost imperceptible. Yet it forms a
watershed.

Southwestwards from the Limousin plateau a series of rivers
run into the Gironde. I shall describe only a small part of them,
for they are the subject of another book of mine called *Three
Rivers of France*. The last little valleys of the Limousin give

1. Castle of Culan

2. Rail and Road Viaducts, Culan

3. The Braggart Lion, Abbey of St.-Amand-de-Boixe

birth to the Charente. It is interesting because it reproduces in miniature the whole river-system of the western and northern Massif. The Charente runs first to the north, in a shallow and secluded valley to Civray, on the southern slope of the Seuil de Poitou. Then it turns right round and wriggles southward to Angoulême. After that it bends westwards with a northerly slant, to the Atlantic Ocean. Now the great Loire and the Allier follow just the same curves, on a far longer course, from the high peaks of the Massif. And so do all the tributaries of the Loire, that rise in the Limousin. The rivers rush swiftly from the plateau in parallel valleys, to slow down in the northern plains, flowing a little west of north till they reach the Loire. The main rivers of this system, east to west, are the Cher, the Indre, the Vienne and its affluent the Creuse. Nearer to the sea the Loire receives another group of rivers, that rise out of the northern side of the limestone plateau of Poitou; or from among the little hills of the Vendée; they are the Thouet and the Sèvre-Nantaise.

The boundary and master of all this land is the Atlantic Sea. Here, as it stretches north to south, it was till recently for the peoples of Europe not only the end of France, but the end of the earth. Here the rollers run with the tides, eating away the margins of the bays, or piling them with sand, so that the shores are perpetually on the move. Here live the people of the sea, whose markets are the towns inland, whose summers are visited by swarms of tourists, but whose way of life is totally different, and is their own.

Chapter Two

THE CHER

1. BERRY

The Cher Valley forms the eastern boundary of this book. The long river rises far over the plateau of the Limousin, near to its junction with the volcanic ranges of the Mont-Dore massif. Thence it meanders northward across the boggy heights, and collects its tributary the Tarde, before seeking the slope down to the limestone rim of the hills from Montluçon to St.-Amand. After that it runs slow in the plains to Vierzon, where it makes the westward curve typical of this system of rivers. At last it joins the Loire, some kilometres west of Tours, at Cinq-Mars.

The modern names for the plain-country are 'Cher' and 'Cher-et-Loire'. The older one still used by the people is Berry. Its capital was for long supposed to be the centre of France, but the geographers have pin-pointed this at Saulzais-le-Potier, a village to the south of Bourges. It remains true that Berry is the heart of France. It is a quiet rolling country with a lot of cattle-farming, a little winegrowing, some industry in the towns, a good deal of forest or near-forest, and on the east side separating it from the Loire, the swampy Solonge.

British and American tourists will come from the north, and I assume that they will take the road from Tours on the south side of the Cher. Now the Loire is excluded from my tale, but I am bound to point out that the prettiest of all the castles that figure in guide-books to the Loire belongs to the Cher. Chenonceau is built on bridges over the river. I shall not attempt to describe the exquisite château, except to record a fact that is less often mentioned than its ownership by one uncrowned queen, Diane de Poitiers, and two crowned queens, Catharine de Medici and Louise de Lorraine. This is that it was built by the wife of a minister of finance, and forfeited after his death by Francis I on the accusation of corruption. That is a recurrent theme in French history, and seems to have been an inexpugnable defect in the working of the monarchy. The visitor will meet it again and again, not least in Berry. Two little towns of the lower Cher are good places to spend the night; they are Montrichard and St.-Aignan,— the latter has a beautiful church, too.

At Selles, a small place where there is an interesting church, and a castle which is not shown but where you can park in the grounds, a main road comes in from Blois, and continues south to Valençay. That château counts among the great castles; but it is not open to the public; you may however walk in its park and see a small museum of souvenirs of Talleyrand. If you share the taste of many diplomats, you may meditate in admiration on the career of this man; if you do not, at any rate you can be fascinated by a mind as intricate as the pillar-carvings of the churches in the Perigord of his ancestors.

The roads on either side of the river are not especially interesting hereabouts because they are made at some distance from the water. Floods inundate the lower ground, and the roads run along the slightly higher ridges that mark the prehistoric banks where far greater rivers flowed, long ago. Between St.-Aignan and Montluçon the Cher is doubled by the Canal de Berry, one of the complex of canals made by the French in the days before railways, when the long distances between markets were traversed by the river-valleys. The rivers themselves were not easy to navigate, because of floods, shoals, and unhelpful winds. Horses were not strong enough for heavy freights, though of course they could carry the small merchants' packs. So the whole of France is threaded by canals. They are still in use today, and they are a great advantage to the holiday-maker, for they leave the rivers themselves free for bathers, fishers, and campers.

The Cher

Vierzon, where the Yèvre flows into the Cher, is an industrial town, notable for the frescoed church of Brinay, some miles away. It is the chief place of the Solonge, the region lying between the Cher, the Yèvre and the Loire. This swampy triangle was, till lately, stagnant and feverish, its peasants very poor. Recently there has been a good deal of drainage, and cultivation is increasing, but earlier there was little to commend the Solonge save an abundance of fish and game. But the little town of Aubigny is of especial interest to Scots. The story began when the King of France, in dire straits after Agincourt, appealed to his ally the King of Scots. The Scottish Council sent a volunteer army under three nobles, who won the first victory of the Valois in 1421 at Pont-de-Beaugé in Anjou. The advantage of that victory was cancelled by the crushing defeat, at Verneuil, of a second army under the Earl of Douglas. Charles VII, still called the Dauphin, gave estates to the Scots leaders; to the Douglas the Duchy of Touraine—much to the disgust of the Tourangeaux—and Aubigny to John Stuart, a kinsman of the Scottish king. The Stuarts d'Aubigny settled in France and became a line of soldiers. The church of Aubigny holds their family memorials, and the pretty Renaissance castle of la Verrerie, near by, has 1421 engraved on its lintel in memory of Beaugé. Now that was eight years before Jeanne d'Arc appeared from Domremy to inspire the royalist French to resistance. There were two other results of the rescue-operation of the Scots. One was the formation of the Scottish Archers, the personal bodyguard of the French kings for three centuries. The huge castle of Maubranche near Bourges was built by one of their early commanders. The Royal Scots, the First of the Line and the oldest of the regiments of the British army, trace their history to the Scottish Archers. The people of Edinburgh, in fond irony at this proud claim to ancientry of their local regiment, call the Royal Scots 'Pontius Pilate's Bodyguard'. The second result of those desperate years was the decree by Charles VII that all Scots should be French citizens, an edict repeated by his son Louis XI. This decree has never been rescinded, so that all Scots can claim French nationality, though I have never heard what would happen if one did so.—It is a nice gambit in conversation with French acquaintances, I have found. Of course, no Frenchman has ever heard of it, any more than French children are taught the story of Pont-de-Beaugé at school.

The people of France have long forgotten the 'Auld Alliance'. Their consciousness of it has shrunk to a vague memory that Mary Queen of Scots, a queen in exile, was married to Francis II and for the brief period of his reign queen of France also. Of course we Scots remember far better. We know that we owe our mediaeval civilization largely to France. (It was not much, perhaps, but for what it was!) The older Scottish towns are far liker to French towns than to English. It was no accident that when the Reformation spread to Scotland the people did not adopt, like the English, the cloudy thought of Luther, but the steely logic of Jean Calvin, that most French of Frenchmen, whose disciple was John Knox. His austere argument appealed to something deep in likeness between the two nations, a likeness of intelligence which still, after centuries of separation and even at times of enmity, causes us to train our children in ways perceptibly more European than do the English, and enables us to make friends far more readily with the French.

Love between nations, like love between man and woman, is never an even exchange. As the French say, 'There is always one who kisses, and one who offers the cheek.' There is no doubt that the Scots love the French more warmly than the French do the Scots. Our mutual debt cannot be balanced. It is idle even to try to assess it. Can we set our culture of the Middle Ages, our towered castles, so closely copied from those of France, the majesty of Edinburgh, that was French before it was Italian, our tradition of the Roman Law, our marvellous cakes that old-fashioned folk still call 'pastry'—'*pâtisserie*'—against the Scots who fell in the service of France, the men who guarded the uneasy sleep of French kings, above all the stricken field of Flodden in 1513, which not only cost us our king and almost the whole of the Scottish chivalry, but ruined our budding Renaissance for ever? We still sing 'The flowers of the forest are all wede awa', but the French have no song to match it. What remains between us? The feeling of recognition, of friendship not yet made, but which can easily be made, that moves us as our eyes meet.

Few of my readers will be Scots. And even Scots may find this long digression tedious. I must apologize to them, pleading that it is an attempt, in the French manner, to reason out a life-long love-affair with France.

Many travellers, however, will find their minds occupied, on the road up the Cher, with thoughts of France herself. France, they are likely to notice, is a vulnerable land. For all her compact shape, squared between the Alps, the Pyrenees, the three seas, she lies open to attack, from the south and the east. Berry, in the centre, lies in the shelter of the Massif Central. But the invader can come—has often come—up either side of the Massif, up the Rhone-Saone gap or by the western plains. And from the north and east you could march from the Urals to Bourges by plains only interrupted by the Ardennes, so easy to circumvent, as the Germans have proved in two invasions of this century. True, the plains are traversed by rivers. But rivers can be crossed by ford, ferry, or bridge. Many Frenchmen cling to a myth of what they call 'the natural frontier', by which they mean the Rhine. But the Rhine is no better a natural boundary than the Somme. It has never proved a lasting hindrance to the advance of invading nations, since the Gauls crossed it eight centuries before Christ. And today to include a Fifth Column of the solidly German population of the Rhineland in France would be madness.

So here we are, like the migrant hordes, in the heart of France. Here came the Romans in 52 B.C. when the Bituriges, the Gauls of the country, dared to resist Julius Caesar and to defend Bourges. That cold genius was merciful or merciless exactly as suited his purpose. When Bourges fell, he killed every man who had borne arms against him. The mark of four centuries of Roman rule is to be seen everywhere in this country, from walls and camps to vineyards and the Christian religion. Yet even in the early days the Romans were forced to fortify the line of the Rhine, part of that long, long line of the 'Limes' that began at Hadrian's Wall and stretched to the Ten Cities of the Syrian Desert. And from time to time it was broken, when the Empire shuddered and split under the blows of the barbarians, while within the line of forts the rival Caesars fought for power, and used the legions to support their ambitions instead of manning the defences.

For a while, the barbarian incursions were temporary, as were those of the Allemans, and of the Huns under Attila in the third century. But behind the raiders came the settlers, pressed to the West by the hungry tribes at their backs. Then the Rhine frontiers broke for the last time, the legions marched away; and France fell piecemeal under the sway of Teutonic nations. Burgundians took the east to the Rhone, Visigoths ruled the west and centre right up to the Loire. In from the north-east came the Franks, fighting tribes bringing their women with them and settling as they conquered.

None of the many historians who have chronicled the barbarian invasions is able to assess the resulting mingling of population. There must have been a great deal of racial admixture from the first, since the women, as is usual in war, were raped and enslaved by the victors. But even the Franks, by far the most savage, needed to preserve the cultivation of the farms to feed their followers. One historian reckons that they used to leave a third of the tilled land in the hands of the Gauls. This may seem rapacious, till it is compared with the proportion of land left to the native peoples of America, Australia, and Africa by European settlers of recent times.

There are some signs to guide the explorer in those jungles of the Dark Ages. One is the gradual adoption of the Christian faith by the barbarians. The Gauls, as a whole, had become Roman Catholics under the Empire. The Visigoths had accepted the Arian creed, which was that of the Emperors of Constantinople at the time of their westward trek. They had also learned Roman law, the Theodosian code, and applied it in Gaul. The Franks, on the contrary, in so far as they adopted Christianity, were Roman Catholics. They learned this creed from the conquered Gauls, after Clovis appealed to the Christian God of his Catholic wife to win him the battle of Tolbiac in 496. This conversion did not affect his way of acquiring the lands of his kinspeople by treachery and murder. But it encouraged the Roman Catholics of the south to ask him to help them against the Arian Visigoths. His victory at Vouillé in 507 gave him the mastery of most of Aquitaine. The other clue to the survival of the Gauls is linguistic. The Teutons of the east continued to use Germanic dialects. Those to the west adopted the demotic Latin that had become the language of camp and market over the centuries. South of the Loire this developed into the Langue d'Oc, a familiar and flexible Romance language; while in the lands dominated by the Franks men spoke the more formal and grammatical tongue of the Langue d'Oil. It is fair, therefore, to assume that the Franks thinned out towards the south and west. To this day the people of the South-West are apt to tell you that they are Gallo-Romans.

The country south of the Loire was contested for centuries, between Franks and Visigoths, between the Merovingian Frankish kings who carved up the country this way and that. Berry was not then a central land, but for a thousand years a frontier country. It is significant that the next province to the west of Berry is called 'Marche': the Border. The Gauls of Berry tended to return to the connection of Aquitania Prima, Bourges, with its old partner Aquitania Secunda, Bordeaux. But by the time that the feudal system had divided all France into lordships belonging to their seigneurs, as they in turn were the vassals of their overlords, eastern Berry had become the County of Bourges, and western Berry part of the immense Duchy of Aquitaine.

This must be told because it explains the later history of Bourges. A Count of Berry was bent upon going on Crusade. He had not enough money to pay his followers, and he sold his lands to the French king in 1101. When he returned from the East, he became a monk. After the sale Bourges was a royal domain, which the kings could govern directly, or grant as an 'apanage' to one of their family. By 1101 the kings of France were the Capets, who had usurped the throne from the decadent Carolingians. So small were the Capet possessions, a strip from Paris to Orleans, that the purchase of Bourges doubled their lands.

I tell this tale of the crusading Count because justice is due to all men. We are accustomed to think of the Crusades as aggressions, led by men greedy for land, and waged with brutality and treachery. This cannot have been true of all crusaders. For some the ideal of the Holy War was a matter of religion; and in the absence of detail one is probably justified in believing that the Count of Bourges went to the Holy Land in good faith, sacrificing his heritage, even if he returned ruined, perhaps broken by experiencing the horrors of crusade, to seek peace in a monastery at the end.

2. BOURGES. THE CATHEDRAL

Bourges is a beautiful city. It is built between the Yèvre and the Auron, on a bluff that rises up to an oval *enceinte* surrounded by the remnants of the Gallo-Roman walls. It is crowned by the Cathedral of Saint-Étienne.

This is an early Gothic cathedral. I have visited it seven times, over many years, and it always makes the same impression. Outside, the building is very complex, for the east end and both sides are netted in flying buttresses, light, lovely, yet conveying their function of supporting the pillars of the nave and aisles within. There are two towers at the west end, one taller than the other. The west end itself is covered with carvings. Five great portals occupy the whole façade. The centre door is surmounted by a great Last Judgment. The pediment holds a Christ in Judgment. Below runs a frieze of the saved and the damned. Saint Michael stands in the midst, holding his scales to weigh good deeds against sins. There is a small imp trying to pull down the scale of sin, but Michael smiles—his arm is round the shoulder of the little soul he is trying. The sculptures have been a good deal restored, but the total effect is authentic.

Enter the door, and the impression is totally different. The church is filled with simplicity and peace. This is due in part to its width. The nave is flanked on either side by two aisles, each much less in height than the other. The arch of the roof is slightly pointed, and the whole is like the hull of a great ship turned upside down, a nave truly. Mainly however the tranquil feeling of Saint-Étienne is due to its uninterrupted space. There are no transepts to break the fourfold line of the pillars. There is no intrusive choir-screen. There was originally a Romanesque *jubé* transferred from an earlier building, but the canons of the eighteenth century destroyed it and replaced it by a classical screen. The Revolutionaries broke this up; how rarely does it happen, and one can be grateful to the outbreaks of mob-violence to which the French are liable! So the visitor sees the whole long church from portal to altar.

I remember once attending on a festival occasion, and watching the service from the western door; for the cathedral was packed with people. Far away, several priests, dressed in splendid robes, knelt, passed, crossed each other in their stately ceremonial dance. They were like an illuminated missal, against the morning splendour of the windows.

The windows of Bourges are glorious. The best, those of the chapels round the apse, are surpassed only by the windows of Chartres. It is believed that they came from the Chartres workshops. Chartres Cathedral is a Sainte-Marie, and the dominant colour of its windows is the blue of the Virgin's robe. Saint-Étienne's windows are chiefly red, the red of the martyr's blood. It is more than a colour; it is like the heart of a furnace, a blaze. The apse and the four aisles all have rows of windows, dating from the twelfth to the fifteenth century. The windows of the tall apse, very high, are giant figures of prophets and apostles. Failing unusually long sight, one must study those with binoculars; in any case they are nothing like so lovely as the small chapel lights. There is one window dating from the nineteenth century, where, on the entrance to its embrasure, is pinned an indignant little note, saying that this window was placed there in 'that base age', '*cette basse âge*'. However, there is no need to look at it, after all.

In the Lady Chapel at the east end there are kneeling statues of Duke Jean de Berry and his second wife Jeanne de Boulogne. A print of a Fouquet drawing of the Duchess lies beside her effigy; in fact the heads are reproductions, that of the Duke of a Hans Holbein drawing.

You can climb the taller of the towers, and get a clear view of the spider-web of the old streets, and of the flat marshy country round the town.

3. THE MAID AND THE GUIDE

I was doing my hair in my room at the Boule d'Or, when the chambermaid knocked and asked if she might make the bed. 'Of course,' said I, and we engaged in polite conversation. She was a child, about sixteen, I thought, watching her in the looking-glass. She was fair, thin, gawky—what did her long-boned face and silky straight hair remind me of?—I got it; she was the Lady of the Unicorn, the girl of the most famous tapestry of France, who stands among all the riches of the seven senses, saved from their temptation by her purity. She is attended with devotion by the Unicorn. I have long thought that that maiden (and many a maiden in many a church) was the ideal of mediaeval aristocracy, withdrawn, sensitive, rather languid. 'That girl is a Frank,' I thought.

The child turned to me, a pillow clasped to her breast, her bony wrists and hands in a Gothic attitude. 'I must tell you Madame', she said, 'I adore your Queen Élizabet! I think she is the most beautiful, the best person in the world!'

I made a reply which I hoped combined loyalty and sense in reasonable proportions; my mind performing meanwhile one of those complicated syntheses that seem to cover a great deal of thought in a flash. 'Especially one owes reverence to children,' I reflected. 'That young girl does not only have the Frankish face of the Lady of the Unicorn, but her dreams too, in these wide-set grey eyes. She has the capacity to spend her life dreaming, in imagination, in introspection, in hero-worship—all that goes to make the Teutonic soul. And why not? At her age, I dreamed of Jeanne d'Arc by night and thought of her by day; what is the difference?' I could only wish this dreamer luck, and at the end of all her successive hero-worships, a kind husband who would bring her gently down to earth.

'This time I shall get into the crypt,' I told myself firmly. 'I am here for a week; it must be open some time.' For on six previous visits the cathedral crypt had been shut. I was bent on seeing it, partly out of simple frustration, but mainly because it contains a

statue, the contemporary grave-stone of Duke Jean de Berry.
Jean de Berry exercises a strong fascination over me. He was the
son of the king Jean le Bon, served and was taken prisoner with
his father at the battle of Poitiers in 1356, and was a hostage
for the king in England for a time. Then he was replaced by a
brother and returned to rule his domains of Berry and Auvergne
for the next sixty years. He was a master-builder and a patron of
art. His architects made wonderful palaces at Paris, Poitiers,
Bourges, Riom, Mehun-sur-Yèvre. At Mehun he had a library
whose illuminated manuscripts are among the finest treasures
of France; they include the 'Très Riches Heures du Duc de
Berry' now at Chantilly. All this work of building, all the artists
and sculptors, had to be paid for, and it was the people who
paid. Nobody has ever called Jean de Berry a good ruler. He was
rapacious; the people said that no widow's portion nor orphan's
heritage was spared from the utmost due. Yet in the time of defeat
of the Valois, the domains that he had governed, descended to his
great-nephew Charles VII, were almost the sum of French lands
that Charles, the 'King of Bourges', could rely on for support.

The statue in the Lady Chapel is b sed upon a drawing by Holbein. Here was no long-nosed suspicious Capet, but a man with a
broad flat face, a pug nose, and eyes twinkling with wit. The
mouth, in contrast, is thin-lipped and pursed, a greedy parrot-
mouth. Jean lived to see France defeated at Agincourt, and many
of his great possessions lost. On that tombstone in the crypt is
engraved, 'See what an illustrious birth, riches and glory serve. I
possessed them for an instant. Now, they escape me.' He left the
palace at Mehun with its marvellous library to Charles, his great-
nephew. It was there that the king loved to live with his kind
mistress Agnès Sorel; it was there that he starved himself to death,
because he believed that his son Louis was determined to poison
him.

Nothing is left of that palace, save a single tower, and nothing
at all of the palace of Bourges, and its jewel of a Sainte-Chapelle.
They were demolished by the canons of the eighteenth century,
slaves to the classical mode.

In the cathedral, the sacristan was engaged in serving the Mass of a visiting priest in a side-chapel. There were two women guides. I asked one if I could see the crypt. She blanched, and told me that I must ask her colleague. There were two priests waiting before the High Altar, one elderly and benevolent, the other young and earnest. I joined them and stood behind them, while the senior guide came up the nave. She was a short old lady, cubically formed, bearing a white wand. The younger priest advanced to meet her and make our request. He returned with a scared face. '*Elle refuse!*' he said. The two collogued, I heard the word '*le Cardinal*' recurring in their consultation. The older priest went forward, his mien combining affability and authority. She raised her voice to deny him access. 'The crypt is shut. It is in the hands of the Ministry of the Beaux Arts. The architect of the Beaux Arts has the key.' I thought: 'This Cardinal cannot be the Cardinal-Archbishop of Bourges, who can surely command entry into his own cathedral-crypt. This must be one from somewhere else.' The elder priest said, 'But the Cardinal has come expressly to see the crypt. Could you not telephone the office of the architect of the Beaux Arts to ask the architect for the key?' 'Well!—I could telephone, I suppose,' said the alarming guide, and stumped off in the direction, presumably, of her post. As she went she turned her head on her shoulder, and fired a Parthian shot. 'The architect will not be in his office,' she said in a triumphant voice.

I went sadly away to look once more at the windows of the east end. 'In any case,' I tried to console myself, 'I could not have joined the party. Priests, yes. But a Cardinal, no. Even the brazen face of a one-time journalist would not give me the impudence to tag after a Prince of the Church.'

So I was foiled again. And I am prepared to wager a moderate sum that the Cardinal was foiled too.

4. THE CITY OF BOURGES

The cathedral is only the beginning of the delights of Bourges. It lies across the Gallo-Roman *enceinte*, the bottom of whose walls is still to be seen here and there between houses. Between them and the vanished longer mediaeval walls run the lively streets with an astonishing number of houses of the Middle Ages and of the Renaissance. The best of all—they say the best in all France—is the house of Jacques Coeur. This is an urban palace, a great merchant's *hôtel*. The entrance is through a portal leading to a series of inner courts and towers, part of them a dwelling-house and part warehouses and offices. The quadrangles are small and enchanting. From simulated windows carven personages look down on the people in the courts. Within, the lintels, the fireplaces, the chapel, are covered with carvings, many of them illustrating the life of the people in the fifteenth century. Mottoes, also, such as the punning '*A coeur vaillans rien impossible*'. I like best the relief of the merchant's two-master, manned with soldiers at poop and forecastle, sailing to Alexandria and the ports of the Levant.

Jacques was the first, and perhaps the greatest, of the financiers who from century to century sustained the fortunes of the French kings. He was a silversmith, a merchant, an industrialist, a landowner, a ship-owner. But for his gifts of money, freely offered, Charles VII could not have paid his army to invade Normandy. He was favoured by lovely Agnès Sorel, the mistress of Charles's later years. Envious courtiers caballed against him and got him accused of malversation. Even though the charges were certainly false, he was tried, threatened with torture, condemned to death. Only the intervention of the Pope saved his life—a protection which may have been due to the circumstance that the son of Jacques Coeur was Archbishop of Bourges at the time. All his wealth was forfeited to the crown, and he died in exile in the Greek islands, commanding a Papal ship.

I wrote that this tale of ministers of finance recurs in French history, with their wealth and their fall on accusation of corruption. Later the memory of Jacques Coeur was vindicated, as was that of Jeanne d'Arc, who lived in Bourges for the winter before her capture by the Burgundians. Charles VII had the nickname of *le Bien-Servi*, the well-served, and that was a true word. Jeanne d'Arc and the Bastard Dunois, Agnès Sorel and Jacques Coeur—the weak and likeable king knew how to enlist faithful servants, and never knew how to be faithful himself. He did not lift a finger to save Jeanne, or Jacques Coeur, the two to whom he owed his throne.

A walk in Bourges is bound to be slow. Partly because the narrow old streets are clotted with traffic, partly because there is so much to look at. The doors have carved tops, the façades of many houses are adorned with saints. The museum is in a Renaissance hotel. The Hotel de Lallemont was built by a merchant who believed that he could find the Philosopher's Stone. It is carved with the Boule d'Or and other symbols of alchemy, and holds what is called a laboratory but which looks suspiciously like a temple of magic. Banks are housed in seventeenth-century stone buildings, shops in brick-and-timber gabled houses. Even the post office is a carefully imitated Renaissance château. The town council keeps a firm hand on new building, and sees to it that neither in height nor in style does it spoil the beautiful town. Outside the line of the walls, modern and totally insignificant flats and offices are allowed to proliferate.

The jewel of Bourges is the Cathedral, set like a ruby on its summit. The setting of the jewel is worthy of that great ruby.

5. THE UPPER CHER

The roads round Bourges carry the mark of the Roman Empire far more notably than the Gallo-Roman *enceinte*. Below the city the land is flat as a pancake, and running with the water of river and swamp. Roads run straight across the plain like the spokes of a wheel. There are nine main roads, and they are marked on maps drawn long before the days of tarmac, or of Napoleon either. There is one to the south-west, for instance, that runs across the farming-land of Berry. It leads to Issoudun, a charming old town, centred on an immense cattle-market, and dominated by a tall mediaeval tower called La Tour Blanche. That remembers Blanche of Castile, the grand-daughter of Henry II of England and Anjou. When she married Louis VIII of France, her uncle John, Duke of Aquitaine and King of England, gave her Issoudun as a dowry, so that all Berry was united as the possession of the French kings.

But the most attractive of the roads run south to the Limousin heights. There are a number of castles roughly centred on St.-Amand-Montrond. The château of Meillant is a perfect example of the high Renaissance *manoir*. It has a beautiful decorated tower, fine state rooms and a flamboyant chapel. It was one of the castles belonging to the family of Amboise, which figures so often in the history of Louis XII. The prettiest road south follows the Cher, on which is built the imposing castle of Châteauneuf, with some good portraits in its Louis XV rooms. But the small castle of Ainay-le-Vieux is by far the most picturesque in this neighbourhood. It is a complete circle of moated walls. You can walk all round them from one tower to the other by the *chemin-de-ronde*, the passage for archers behind the battlements. The latest tower is of the Renaissance, and some rooms are shown. They contain a number of Napoleonic relics. For the owner was one of Napoleon's generals. He committed the impolicy of welcoming back the Emperor from Elba, and was cast into prison after Waterloo. This naturally promoted him to martyrdom, and assured the devotion of his family to the Napoleonic party from that day to this.

I mean here to digress on a personal note. Ours is an age of brutal and senseless wars. The effect on me, a student of history old and new, is to cause me to reflect on the men whose fame rests on their success as war-makers. The great conquerors have almost always been insane with pride and greed. They have believed that their victories justified the destruction of thousands of men's lives; those of their opponents and their followers. Napoleon was typical. He reduced not only all Europe, but France itself, to misery and ashes. He was not French, but a Corsican adventurer, but he followed the evil Frankish tradition of aggressive war. He made France, which has hardly yet recovered from his death-roll, the terror of Europe. At Ainay-le-Vieux I looked at his relics with nausea, just as I look, in the library of Edinburgh, at the shelves of books about him. Many men admire him to the verge of worship. To me he was finally described by a young Frenchman, in the course of a lunch-time discussion in an inn; 'Napoleon', he said. '*Un tueur d'hommes.*' 'A man-killer'.

All historians, let alone mere students like me, must choose

4. Farm near Parthenay

5. Gençay. Door Pillars

6. Aulnay. South Door

7. The Cavalier of Parthenay-le-Vieux

some principle from which to judge history. The reader will grant me this right.

The rare thing in this neighbourhood is the Abbey of Noirlac. It is on the Cher road just below St.-Amand-Montrond. It is a great dark bare congeries of buildings, clustered round a church. The abbey stands today much as it did when a kinsman of Saint Bernard of Clairvaux built it. It shows exactly what that Puritan planned in his reform of monasticism. He decreed even the measurements of Cistercian churches, denuded not only of the vain ornaments against which he inveighed so bitterly, but even of complexity of proportion. The walls are of uniform height, the eastern end flat. The monastic buildings are mainly complete, adjoining the plain cloister; kitchen, monks' dormitory, the common dormitory of the lay brothers, or *convers*. This last is much bigger than the quarters of the choir-monks; the guide tells you that there were two hundred brothers and five hundred lay brothers. Above the refectory are the rooms of the abbot, and there, after one's mind has become attuned to austerity, one is fairly startled. For the line of large cells are decorated for comfort, with carved chimney-pieces and alcoves for beds. Then one realizes that these luxuries date from the seventeenth century, long after the 'Commendations' of abbots had been granted to the French kings, who appointed men who were often laymen, and in any case were awarded the abbacies in order that they should enjoy the revenues of the abbey lands.

None the less, what would Saint Bernard have said to all this? The question rises irresistibly in the visitor's mind. But as he looks back from the top of the hill, the impression of the severity of Saint Bernard's religion rules the whole dark abbey.

On the Cher, just above St.-Amand-Montrond, at Drevent, there are the traces of a Roman station. The theatre is carved out of a convenient hillside. The Romans, all over their empire, furnished their military encampments with amenities like theatres and arenas. They were conscious that the life of the stations was boring in the extreme. For the legions were often drawn from distant lands. The military authorities were well aware that bored soldiers sulk and get out of hand. Their engineers and architects were as capable of building theatres as they were of making roads, and a local population furnished an ample supply of slave-labour to do the digging and weight-carrying. The road up the Cher is joined here by a very pretty one up the valley of the Aumance, bordering on the forest of Tronçais, the most beautiful forest of oaks in France. In autumn it is devoted to hunting. It is also, for lovers of that enchanted book, the scenery of *Le Grand Meaulnes* by Alain Fournier.

There is one little place off the Montluçon road to the west, which I insert here because it is difficult to place it. It is Culan, a perched village where a great castle is set above a river-gorge. It is the castle of one of Jeanne d'Arc's friends, the Amiral de Culan; she stayed there for a while. The castle is complete even to the shutters on the crenellations of the battlements, which the archers slammed shut after they fired their arrows. There are two spring-ing viaducts carrying the road and railway, one above the other.

Montluçon is a busy town at the upper end of the Canal de Berry. Its heart is old, containing some ancient houses, and the tight mediaeval town is dominated by a castle, of which the outer wall remains, and from whose terrace there is a fine view.

From Montluçon the main road runs over the hills to Riom and Clermont-Ferrand, in the heart of the Massif Central. But this journey does not go that way, but takes the road up the Limousin by the right bank of the Cher. This road makes continual curves, and switches up and down gaining a little height with each up-ward pull. Presently it runs to the west in watery country; a country of small burns and of lochans. For now it has left the Cher and has joined the Tarde.

Stones, springs, water lying on top of the ground; this is true hill-country. The road reaches Chambon. There is not much beauty about the old town, but there is the church of Sainte Valérie. A pilgrimage to her shrine still takes place every autumn, and fills the vast church. This is a typical Limousin fane, bare, dark, hugely strong. There is a famous reliquary-bust of Sainte Valérie in Limoges enamel in the treasury; but if, as when I visited the church, there is nobody about, you may miss this.

She must have been a well-loved saint. She was a disciple of

Saint Martial of Limoges, and her beheaded body rested at first in his famous abbey. But she proved too well loved; pilgrims came to her shrine rather than to his, and the monks were annoyed. They moved her to the abbey of Solignac near by, and the same thing happened. Pilgrims neglected Saint-Martial and went to Solignac. This was too much; the monks of Saint-Martial despatched the relics up to the small abbey of Chambon in the misty hills. 'And that disposes of Sainte Valérie,' they may have thought. Not so; the people climbed the hills by the narrow paths. It is even possible that they felt that the remoteness of the place, the weariness of the slopes, added to its holiness. The abbey was able to build the great two-towered church. Far away on the Norman coast, there is a village called after Sainte Valérie. The Highland Division, the Fifty-First, was trapped there in 1940. No ships came to rescue the soldiers, as they came to Dunkirk. The Fifty-First, which never surrendered, was forced to surrender. The men danced on the sands, to the pipes, till that hour came. The tune of that dancing is called today the 'Sainte-Valérie Reel'.

Now here is a strange thing. I defy any visitor of Central France to remain indifferent to the names of saints of whom he has heard only vaguely, if at all. Who, for instance, was Saint Léger, when he was not the name of a horse-race? (He was, in fact, a bishop of Poitiers and Autun who was imprisoned and murdered by a Merovingian king.) My habit is to consult two dictionaries of saints contained in the Library of Scotland; one of Jesuit derivation, and the other compiled by the Benedictines of Ramsgate. But the former contains no mention of Sainte Valérie, and the latter remarks austerely, 'This saint probably never existed.' One must respect the scholarship of these learned men, and their reluctance even to chronicle superstition. But while it is likely enough that Sainte Valérie did not rise after her execution, take her head in her hands, and seek her master Saint Martial, this does not alter the fact that pilgrims have sought her shrine for a thousand years, which is surely a piece of history which is worthy of record. Also I think that it is interesting that the Dukes of Aquitaine were crowned in Limoges Cathedral wearing the ring of Sainte Valérie on their hands. Richard Coeur-de-Lion was so crowned.

Near Chambon is Évaux, a cure-place for rheumatic complaints. It has a rather strange church, with a belfry porch. The country round is attractive, for it is unspoiled hill-country running with streams and set with hedges. You can drive over the hills to Gueret or Aubusson on the Indre, but a more interesting route lies over the height to Boussac. This has an ancient castle set high on a cliff over the river Petite-Creuse; a long line of towers. It is finely furnished with antique furniture by its owner. It was there that the tapestries of the Dame à la Licorne were found and taken by the French government to hang in the Cluny Museum at Paris. George Sand protested at this rape in vain. She was a friend of the *châtelain*, and the castle marks the crown of the country of her pastoral novels.

Thus ends the journey up the Cher. It is a peaceful tour, with one great sight, the Cathedral of Bourges, and a number of lesser churches and castles sufficient to satisfy all but ravenous travellers. I like Berry very much for its gentle beauty. Visitors in search of peace could well divide their time between Bourges, and one of the small places deep in the country, like Hérisson on the Aumance, Culan, or Saint-Bonnet-Tronçais among the great oaks of the forest.

8. Lanterne des Morts: Château Larcher, twelfth century

9. Cross of Belle-Croix

Chapter Three

THE INDRE

The Indre, the second river of Berry, parallels the Cher to the west. It is not nearly so long a stream, for it rises on the northern slope of the Limousin, where a number of brooks drain the hillside above St.-Sevère. Then it follows the curve of its basin northwestwards till it meets the small foldings of chalky downs that protect the Loire. Behind them the Indre feels its way till it finds a breach and joins the Loire at Ingrandes. That is a name which in the Celtic speech means 'border'; it can be found in various places where the lands of one tribe met those of another.

Between Indre and Cher lies a rolling plain called 'la Champagne Berrichonne'. It is not interesting country, save for the crops that grow there. They are mainly fodder-crops, oats, beet, the yellow-blooming colza, for this is cattle-country. The big farms lie far apart, each including the farm-workers' cottages or quarters in its group of buildings, so that it is nearly a hamlet. I drove once across the Champagne in early Spring, by the main road from Château-roux to Issoudun. The sound of tractors growled over the fields, and the new-turned earth had the beauty of nakedness. Here and there, where the chalky surface lay over red sandstone soil, the fields looked like raspberries and cream. Where there had been winter sowing, the corn was a veil of green, thin and soft as a baby's hair. I stopped for a picnic by the roadside. The tractors had stopped too. The country was dead silent. Where were the birds? This was hedge and ditch land; where were the thrushes?

It was pasture, there should have been larks. And where were the flowers? I come to France always in early Spring, to see the cowslips. On the verges of roads where cattle have been driven for thousands of years, they grow so thick that they run like a double river beside every track. The air is filled with their scent, velvety and sharp, the very breath of Spring. That morning, there were none. It was a wet cold spring, the spring of 1965, and everything was late. But this blank silent nature chilled the heart. Had the farmers poisoned all the countryside with their weed-killers? Was this Rachel Carson's 'Silent Spring?' I am not sure, for I met nobody to ask. But it is true that I only found the cowslips when I reached forest country on the Limousin, and heard no birds till, in mid-April, I saw the migrants, and heard the cries of the swallows over water, the nightingales startling into bubbling song in the hedges, and a cuckoo singing as he flew across a glade between the trees.

Now if the traveller chooses to follow the Indre, there are four places for him to look at going upstream from the Loire. Near its end the Indre has a castle that rivals Chenonceau, at Azay-le-Rideau. It has the most elegant staircase of all France, save perhaps that of Francis I at Blois. This château too is built actually above the river, on piles. The village has a delightful contrast in the Carolingian west end of the tiny church. It must be one of the oldest buildings in France.

Upstream comes the city of Loches. That is so wonderful a town of the Middle Ages that it is always included in guidebooks to the Loire; but this seems to me no reason for denying it to the honours of the Indre, its own river. It belonged for long to the lands of Anjou where it formed a frontier fortress. Henry II Plantagenet built the great donjon of the castle; which after several changes of hands was lost by John Lackland to Philip Augustus. After that, it was a castle of the French kings, and in the dangerous days of their defeats it was lived in by Charles VII and Agnès Sorel, by Charles VIII and Louis XII. All this tale of history shows in the great castle, looming over the little town from its high rock. That is a long-shaped triangle, guarded by a towered gate. On its top there is room for three castles within the battlemented walls. One, the original Henry II tower, has lost its ceilings, but you can climb it by stairs in the walls and look down at Loches. It is separate from the other castles, which are built on to each other; one a plain fortress where Charles VII lived, the other a Renaissance château with tall gabled windows which was the dwelling of Louis XII. There is a lot to be seen in these castles. The rock itself is riddled with caves and quarries, of which one was used as a secret entrance to the fort. Some of the others are dungeons, especially one where the ill-fated Ludovico Sforza of Milan was imprisoned for eight years after his defeat at Novara. He, who had been the patron of Leonardo da Vinci, painted childish frescos on the walls of his cell in the few hours of daylight. Above that is the cell where Louis XI kept the Cardinal de la Balue for years in a cage. Nobody was more expert at keeping men suspected of treason in gaol than that able but detestable king, who had spent his youth rebelling against his own father. Yet one of the few likeable things I ever read about him concerned his father's love, Agnès Sorel. She was tortured by a sense of sin, and gave generous gifts to the church of the castle, St.-Ours, to ensure that she would be buried there and that the priests would say masses for her soul. But when she died the priests of the collegiate church refused her burial inside its walls. Louis XI flatly blackmailed the Prior. He told him that St.-Ours would get no more support from the crown if they would not let Agnès rest there. They gave way, and her tomb lasted till the Revolution, when some revolutionaries, thinking that it was a statue of the Virgin, smashed it to atoms. A faithful craftsman collected the pieces, and put them together again so perfectly that it is difficult to see the joins. The statue lies now in one of the castle towers. A few of the rooms are arranged as a sort of museum; the most interesting object is the reproduction of a Fouquet portrait of Agnès Sorel as the Virgin Mary; her head is surrounded by a ring of angels—but they are scarlet angels, somewhat sinister. The original picture is in Antwerp. I remember recognizing it from the Loches statue many years before they brought the copy to France; and small credit to me; anybody with eyes in his head must have seen the resemblance. She has a lovely gentle face.

The church is a curious one, roofed with pyramids. But the best thing about the castle is the view from its walls. Below the sheer drop the clustered red roofs of the city rise up. They are mainly of the fifteenth and sixteenth centuries, with pointed gables, though there is one fine Louis XIII street. Across the Indre is the Romanesque tower of the Abbey of Beaulieu, which indeed is best seen from a distance, for when you attain it, it is badly damaged. Loches has another church, St.-Etienne, with a fine triptych by Fouquet; a pretty Renaissance Town Hall, and a decorative Court of Justice in the style of the eighteenth century.

Above Loches, there is a beautiful view of the river from Châtillon-sur-Indre, where an old church and a donjon tower dominate the river-crossing. Some ten miles to the north-east is Nouans-les-Fontaines, whose Romanesque church holds a Descent from the Cross, a Fouquet masterpiece. If you keep to the river the next town is Châteauroux. This is a busy trading town, with few remains of its long history, save parts of the castle englobed in the town hall. But not far south the road runs into the Forest of Nohant, and there begins the realm of George Sand.

I do not know if children are forced to read the pastoral novels of George Sand at school, as I was. They are favoured by teachers, because they are highly moral—though they are earthy too—and because they are written in pure and supple French. George Sand was a forerunner of that loosening of the formality of literary French for which her country owes much to women writers. In this she resembles Colette, who was also, in some of her work, a novelist of the deep country, and who also used the direct speech of country people. Unfortunately George Sand lacked the gift of suspense, so that she bores children. Her books are far more likely to appeal to adult minds, as I found when I rather wearily borrowed some of them from the library. To grownups they are attaching, both because of their clean style, and because George Sand was deeply interested in the ways of the peasant people of Berry. She was lucky in her date of the mid-nineteenth century, for if she had lived today she would almost certainly have been doomed to be a field anthropologist. She would have been a very good one, but it is much pleasanter to learn of the countryfolk by her stories; of the little farm girl who loves the kind ploughman, a widower, and too old for her, (at thirty-two) in *La Mare au Diable*, or of *La Petite Fadette* the half-wild orphan who adores the handsome well-born farmer's son; the tales are full not only of the ways of life but of the morality and sentiment of the villagers, and none the worse for that. But of course the world of her own day, the world of disillusioned Balzac, of her various lovers, including Chopin, laughed at the contrast between George Sand's country novels and her sophisticated life; trousers, cigars, disorder, passionate affections wrecked by passionate quarrels, and all. Another George, her contemporary George Eliot, managed to live with a lover for years in an atmosphere of the gravest respectability. George Sand never achieved that.

At all events she has won the honour of having half the Indre country called after her. As the road goes uphill, it passes first the hamlet of Vicq, which typifies the country in its church. For that is very old, of the twelfth century, and it is entirely covered with contemporary frescos. They are difficult to see unless you open the transept door, but the drawings, of sepia and brown, are really interesting. It is a queer thing, but every saint and Biblical hero has a pronounced squint. Probably this was due to the influence at that time of Byzantine art. For the mosaic persons of Byzantine churches often have squinting eyes, due no doubt to the desire to depict the inward-looking and holy soul, detached from this wicked world.

Nohant is George Sand's own village, where stands her little castle, less a castle than a country manor—a *gentilhommière*, as the French say. The hamlet surrounds a green with a tiny deep-eaved church, a thatched inn that provides excellent food, and the seventeenth-century house. Here George Sand lived with a formidable grandmother who had been the mistress of Eugène de Savoie— and she claimed descent from Charlemagne, no less, though on the wrong side of the blanket. Here her own granddaughter lived till quite recently, and willed the house to the Institut de France.

Inside the gate, the group of tourists must start at a given signal. For this is one of the show-places where the owners have installed a device. The guardian gives you a wireless receiver, like a telephone without its mouthpiece. It is fitted with a strap to hang on your shoulder, leaving your hand free to hold the receiver to your ear. The guardian takes you across a courtyard darkened by overgrown shrubs, through a shadowy hall, and into the dining-room where the table is set with George Sand's china. You are shown all over the house, where the rooms open one into the other in the old fashion. A narrow bare room shelved for manu-scripts is called 'Chopin's Room'. All the time, the machine speaks a script into your ear. It is conveyed rather sentimentally, to be sure, in the sweet voice of some actress. Behind the voice someone plays Chopin, not brilliantly, but adequately, and this is right; for it is used as an accompaniment to the speaking voice. The script gives an overwhelming impression of work, the work over which George Sand took such pains, through all the vicis-situdes of her crowded and stormy life. The account is largely framed of quotations from her journals and letters. 'I am not great' she says with touching humility; 'I have tried to do what I can as well as I could.'

One passes from the bedroom where a big-eyed child visited her fascinating and alarming grandmother in bed for breakfast, to the studio where her son filled cases with his collection of butter-flies, and made the puppets which were his sad attempt to inherit his mother's talent. The script says that at the end of her life, passed in this country, with that wild heart resigned to peace at the last, she occupied herself with helping the peasants, who called her '*la Bonne Dame de Nohant*'. Perhaps it is needless for me to say that the French word '*bonne*' does not translate as 'good'. It means 'kind'. I think that George Sand would have wished for no better title to be remembered by.

All the valley of the Indre upstream from Nohant is called 'the Dark Valley' nowadays, for this is the name with which she en-dowed it, setting her romances in recognizable villages and castles, where her rustic Cinderellas lived their love-stories. You may find references to her all the way up the Indre, by le Châtre, which was her shopping town, to Boussac where she visited and tried to save the Lady of the Unicorn from the clutches of the Cluny.

Chapter Four

CHURCHES AND CHURCH-BUILDING

1. ORIGINS

Here, where the western rise of the Indre valley marks the border between Berry and Poitou, is the time and place to consider churches. For the old art of church-building, throughout the departments of Haute and Basse Vienne, and of the Charentes, fills the eye of the traveller and the mind of the student.

Across the wide plains, down in the steep-sided valleys of the rivers, church-towers rise above the dwellings of the people. Often they stand alone, no house near. The traveller, seeing the round east end, the square tower, says to himself, 'This can't be another!' But it always is; another Romanesque church, built in the eleventh or twelfth century. It may date originally from even earlier, and have a font hollowed in the time of the house of Charlemagne inside it, or a stone coffin of the Merovingian age outside. Many churches have parts added later than the period of Romanesque building. But, in general, the effect is that of the centuries when that style was common to most of France, as it had been much earlier in the Byzantine Empire, and the Italy of the Lombards.

If this book should fall beneath the eye of a learned reader, I should like to say to him 'Please skip this chapter!' I write for ordinary people, not for historians. Most travellers do not know much about architectural history. I propose to give a summary sketch of it as it bears on this region. Nothing would be easier than to allude in a knowing manner to dates and styles, as we were trained to do in our essays at Oxford, because we wanted to show our tutors that we had read the authorities, without boring them with narratives which they knew only too well. But the allusive method, when used in books for normal readers, is maddening. How often I have read in a work of some great author an allusion to a fact of which I knew neither the cause nor the explanation, and been tempted to throw the book across the room!—only I was bred to revere books and am incapable of throwing them anywhere—. So I shall attempt a plain account of the churches of Poitou.

Poitevins take their churches for granted. 'Sixty-four per cent of our churches are Romanesque,' said a professor of the University of Poitiers to me. In Angoumois and Saintonge—which nowadays are called the Charentes—the percentage must be nearer ninety. Even allowing for the tendency of early mediaevalists to include in their reckoning any church of which a fairly large part belongs to their beloved age, the visible facts remain astonishing. Charente counts that it has five hundred Romanesque churches. What would we say if a sizable county in Britain, say Hereford, had five hundred Norman churches instead of a scant handful? We should fill the shire with students and with tourists! The French, except for an arcane company of experts, pay little attention to their treasury of the early Middle Ages. Yet it is true to say that in recent years this period has come into its own, and that an increasing number of scholars are interested in it.

The old churches have been neglected largely because many of them take a good deal of finding. Down the country run the great motorways, wide and horrible, to Bordeaux and the Pyrenean passes, to Royan and les Sables d'Olonne, servicing the summer holiday traffic. They follow the lines of the tracks paved for the Roman legions, tarmac roads now. At the crossroads the Gauls had their tribal centres, the Romans their cities, the feudal seigneurs their castles, the Church its cathedrals. These even the tourists thrusting south by the *routes nationales* cannot miss. They notice that Poitiers is Romanesque, that Saintes is both Roman and Romanesque. But tourists wild for the sea have no time to trace the rivers, to turn aside to tiny villages a mile off the main

10. Tomb statues of Eleanor of Aquitaine and Richard Coeur-de-Lion. Fontrevault Abbey

11. House at Richelieu

road. It is the leisurely who discover with satisfaction, the lovers of the round apse and the carved doorway with rapture, the evidences of an ancient civilization.

Romanesque architecture had certain characteristics wherever it is found. It is rightly named after Rome, for it uses the Roman round arch for roofs and for the tops of doors and windows. In its later stages builders thought of crossing the round arches at junctions, and this produced a pattern of circles cutting each other in sections; and with this the beginning of the style we call Gothic, the age of the pointed arch.

When the Christians were officially tolerated, by Constantine's edict of Milan in 313, they began to build churches. Before that, they had met for prayer in private houses or barns, and had taken to caves and cellars in time of persecution. But when it became safe to build they did not usually imitate the classic temples— though there are churches which are temples adapted to Christian use, like some in Rome. The early builders preferred to copy the basilica, the town hall of the Romans, where they met to transact public business. It had one end reserved for the seats of the elders, the senators. As the Christian churches grew more elaborate, there were many additions to the basic rectangle of the basilica; domed roofs in the East, copied later in western Europe, the habit of setting the altar in the semicircular east end of the church because that was the direction of Jerusalem; transepts between the east end, the apse, and the west end, the nave, which were taken to symbolize the arms of the Cross. Romanesque churches in France may have all these features, or none, save the eastward position of the altar, which is almost invariable.

The greatest difference between the classic temples and the Christian churches is plain to anyone who uses his eyes. Both employ walls and pillars to sustain their roofs. But the temple wears its pillars outside the walls, the church inside. This is not to say that there are no pillars visible on the exterior of churches; many door-frames and window openings are flanked by little pillars; in Poitou the square towers are often composed of ranked pillars, set in stories. But till the high Renaissance, when the Baroque builders included everything the Romans ever thought of, the walls were stone uprights with pillars in lines within to help take the strain of the coverings.

In France, churches dating from before the year 1000 are extremely rare. Poitiers has one, the Baptistery of St.-Jean. Of course there were many churches. But they were frequently destroyed by fire; if, as often happened, they were built of wood, burning was easy. The barbarian invasions were a more thorough form of destruction. Warlike invaders such as the Huns of Attila naturally ravaged the churches. Even after they were superficially converted to Christianity, the Franks were addicted to razing abbeys. The sons of Clovis burned the abbeys of Auvergne, and killed or enslaved the people sheltering in the shrines of Brioude and Mauriac, including the priests. Even the later line of Charlemagne alternated between ruining and founding abbeys, as though on the principle that the merit of the latter atoned for the sin of the former deed. Where the kings led, the nobles followed. Guy-Geoffroy-Guillaume, Count of Poitiers, ravaged the abbey of Luçon, and in expiation built Montierneuf in Poitiers in 1076. The Normans were perhaps the most destructive of all. They were pirates, not settlers, out simply for loot. They devastated every church in the valleys of the Loire and the Garonne, for the sake of their treasures of sacred vessels. Yet once they were bought off by the grant of Normandy in 911, they settled down, abandoned their banditry in France for a strict legality, and confined their rapacity to other lands—England, for instance—. They also became the greatest builders of Romanesque churches, except the Emperors of Byzantium.

Every observant visitor in the French countryside is likely to come across evidence of the decivilization of the barbarian settlements. The grass growing over the Roman cities, because the Franks hated towns and left them to rot; the decay in craftsmanship and learning, so that they almost died out; these continued with only a temporary pause in the reign of Charlemagne. He summoned the monk Alcuin from York to teach him and his family their letters. The English scholar later founded a school of calligraphy at St.-Benoît-sur-Loire; beautiful 'Charlemagne' manuscripts are treasured here and there in France. But it did not last. In the tenth century a monk, Gerbert d'Aurillac, dismayed at the illiteracy of the clergy, put off his robe and went to the Arab kingdoms of Spain, where he passed as a Moslem. He returned having learned the Arabic civilization, then far ahead of that of the Christian lands. In especial, he brought with him the numerals we use today. The people thought him a wizard—in the Middle Ages any man who tried to widen the boundaries of knowledge was considered a warlock—but none the less he became the Pope Sylvester II, the Pope of the Millennium.

Gloom darkened Christendom for long before the year 1000, when all men believed that the world would perish on the Day of Doom. The very people who were professionally concerned with the welfare of the Church, the priests, were too convinced of the imminence of judgment to think of building churches. Why raise walls to fall in ruins?

> *When shrivelling like a parched scroll,*
> *The flaming heavens together roll,*
> *When louder still, and yet more dread,*
> *Swells the high trump that wakes the dead.*

Walter Scott's paraphrase of the Dies Irae expresses the feeling of the time. We who live under the threat of the atom bomb can well understand that apathy which can only formulate philosophies of materialism and despair. Like us, the men of A.D. 999 lay down at night with fear, and rose at dawn with unhappiness.

But the Millennium passed, and the world did not end. The theologians of doom deferred their dark speculations to a term without a date. Meantime the settlement of Normandy had granted France an interval of relative peace, save naturally for the blood-feuds of the nobles. Men tilled the fields again, and felled the forests. Trade picked up slowly. In the immense relief of the continuing world, there was a great religious revival, with a renewal of the priestly and monastic vocations, and men built the Romanesque churches.

Raoul Glaber, a Cluniac monk, wrote a chronicle which gives us the best contemporary evidence. He died about 1050. All French historians quote him, and I have done so myself in another book.

'So on the threshold of the aforesaid thousandth year, some two or three years after it, it befell throughout the world, but especially in Italy and Gaul, that the fabrics of churches were rebuilt, although many of them were still seemly and needed no such care. But every nation rivalled with the other which should worship in the seemliest buildings. So it was as if the world had shaken herself and cast off her old age, and were clothing herself everywhere in a white veil of churches. Then indeed the faithful rebuilt and bettered all the cathedral churches and other monasteries, dedicated to divers saints, and smaller parish churches.'

Glaber goes on to say that many relics were discovered, 'revealed by divers proofs and testimonies'. Testimonies, no doubt; proofs—well, possibly not so trustworthy. A church was always dedicated to a patron, ranging from the Holy Trinity down to a local saint. And it was bound to try to obtain a relic, a tomb, or a bone, or a scrap of stuff, to justify the name and perhaps to attract pilgrims. There was, of course, a long-established custom of the reverence of relics. As to their discovery, opinions varied, but few doubted their value to the churches.

2. THE CARVED CHURCHES OF AQUITAINE

When this wave of building flooded over France, the builders developed local groups. This was inevitable. Distances were immense, reckoned in time taken to cover them. The various provinces were ruled by lords so powerful that they were really small kings. Not so small either. The Dukes of Aquitaine, sovereign over France from the Atlantic to the Cevennes, were many times more powerful and rich than the Capets, the somewhat upstart dynasty whose founder had been elected by a packed council of peers. The Capets were the anointed kings, to be sure, and the *sacre* entitled them to the homage of all the tenants-in-chief; but they only owned a strip of land from Paris to Orleans, where they had difficulty in getting their own vassals under control. The Dukes of Aquitaine had plenty of turbulent vassals too, but all through their vast territories men could come and go, and seigneurs, bishops and abbots could exchange news about the

12. St. Piere-de-Chauvigny. Pillar-Capital of the Dancer

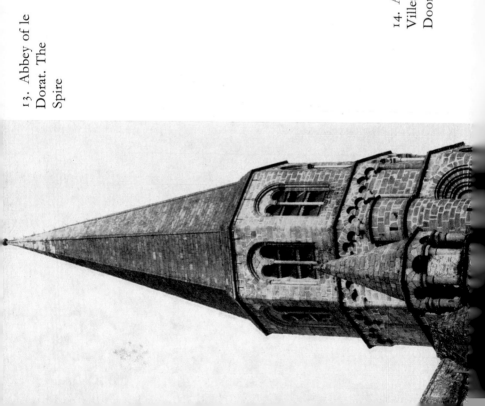

13. Abbey of le Dorat. The Spire

14. Abbey of Villesalem. Door

new churches. It was especially important that they spoke the Langue d'Oc, for language is the foundation of a shared civilization. Even within the bounds of Aquitaine, there were local schools of architecture. Périgord, for instance, favoured domes for the roofs of churches. But if a religious leader from far away on the borders of Anjou liked domes, there was nothing to prevent him from choosing them, as Robert d'Arbrissel's followers chose domes for the Abbey of Fontrevault.

The heart of the Gallo-Roman country round Poitiers, reaching from Thouars in the north to Saintes in the south, had a different idiom. Experts, indeed, can distinguish between the churches of Poitou and those of Angoumois and Saintonge. But the likenesses are far greater than the differences. And the first thing that they seem to share is their gentleness. Romanesque fanes are often terrifying; in Poitou they are tender.

The stone of which they are built, throughout the limestone lands, is beautifully coloured. Limestone, the petrified bones of prehistoric fishes, is basically white. But the minerals present in the lime dye it with many tints. The churches may be deep cream. amber, russet. Occasionally their surface is like the petals of a pale rose, sometimes like the skin of a deer.

The soft stone lends itself to carving, and it is the ornament that gives its specific character to the churches of the region. This also is the main clue to the builders themselves; for who they were remains mysterious. Some have thought that they were monks, and various stories suggest that abbots 'built' their monasteries. No doubt they supervised the building strictly. It seems likely however that like the lords who are also recorded as building churches, this was a matter of ordering them—and paying for them. For there are so many churches, and so many sculptures, that it seems far more probable that there was a strong skilled craft of building, within which the stone-masons and the erectors worked in cooperation with the carvers. The later Gothic builders of cathedrals are so depicted, for instance in one of the windows of Bourges. Few visitors can fail to notice the brand of professionalism borne by those churches. The doors have been shaped to fit the carved rings of their vaults. I should have loved to go round a few of them with a modern building mason, but I never had the luck. He would have seen so much that I missed.

The sculptures form a school of their own. They vary from mere geometric outlines like those incised on ancient pottery to bewilderingly elaborate decoration. The façades, the west ends of some churches, are like curtains of carving hung before the walls. They encircle the windows and portals, they run in friezes across the whole width of the front. The lovely east ends too, rounded to enclose the altar-apse, and often surrounded by a covey of smaller and lower semicircles formed by chapels in the interior, are carved in arches and bands. The edges of the roofs are supported by corbels to help balance the strains of the vaults. These are usually carved hilariously as devils or beasts. Inside, the pillars that form the aisles in the nave, and that often encircle the altar, are almost always topped by carven capitals.

This sculpture has two lines of development. The simplified carving of small village churches may be simply due to poverty, for at the same time great churches are often being covered with quantities of detailed work. Also, of course, the carving grew more technically skilled and finished with time; it was always small in scale, but it became more and more delicate and elaborate, till, like all schools of art, it reached a perfection from which there was no way forward but to decay.

3. TYPES OF CARVING

The subjects of the carvings fall into classes. There are the outline geometrical designs, which developed into 'repeat' patterns, like serrations, or basket work. There are plants and leaves—flowers are rare except the Oriental marguerite. Plants are found specially in the pillar-capitals, where the acanthus of the classic temples is varied by palm-leaves and buds. The most beautiful of these 'vegetable ornaments' as one guide-book calls them, are to my mind the 'Aquitanian interlacings', *les entrelacs aquitains*. These are endlessly intertwined and fantasticated, breaking out into animal forms. The eye cannot follow them from end to end. They resemble the initial letters of monkish illuminations, or the carved crosses of Scotland, or Oriental rug-patterns. It is perhaps because I am a Scot, and familiar with the interlacings, that I prefer them to all other Romanesque sculptures.

But many will like the animals better. They are sometimes naturalistic—at least one can suppose the innumerable lions to be attempts at naturalism. Yet even the lions are often humanized, as is the vainglorious Lord Lion of my illustration, who, I am sure, is the caricature of a seigneur. There are many birds. The pair of peacocks confronting each other on either side of a tree or vine are among the most persistent Christian symbols; they are found in the carvings of Byzantium; they are painted today upon pottery in the island of Rhodes. I remember a Yugoslav refugee of the First World War, whom I was watching at her loom, explaining to me that they meant the immortality of the soul, feeding on the True Vine.

Far more of the animal forms are stylized monsters. There are dragons and harpies, and what the experts sometimes, in desperation, call 'Quadrupeds'. There is the strangest of all, the Griffin. You may not recall the nature of this monster, and no more did I, till I looked him up in an encyclopaedia. He has the beak and claws of an eagle, the ears of a horse, the neck of a swan, the body of a lion, the wings of a hawk, the tail of a snake. All that, and a sort of simple good-nature too. Sometimes the swan neck is twisted to enable him to pick fleas off his back, but I do not recall him devouring a lost soul, like a lion or a dragon. He is my favourite monster, for he stirs compassion in the heart for his very ugliness, his grotesqueness of the eternal clown. He is very old. I am told there is a splendid prehistoric griffin in the museum of Teheran; the Greek museums have little bronze griffin medals which scholars think were the guild badges of Parthian merchants. I have a private fancy, with no justification whatever, that I can recognize the work of a carver whom I call 'the Master of the Griffin' in the Aquitanian churches.

Lastly there are the carvings of human forms. They are as stylized as the animals. They are small, with hardly expressed character in their faces. Even Delilah holding Samson's severed hair in her hands is merely careful. One recognizes the figures of the Scriptures by their attributes. Christ in glory sits with the heavenly footstool of the world beneath His feet. Peter is crucified upside-down. The Elders of the Apocalypse are often used as a frieze or border, the book in one hand, the phial in the other, the Virgin Mary is rarely present, still more rarely very important, despite the frieze of her ancestry at Ste.-Marie-la-Grande at Poitiers. The age of adoration of the Virgin was not yet. Sometimes saints confront devils; often men are devoured by the Deadly Sins. Two stories are favoured, because they make such good margins for an arched doorway. One is the Wise and Foolish Virgins, up the right side cherishing their lamps, down the left side desperately begging for lights—as ever the heart goes out to the Foolish Virgins, the Wise ones are so mean. The other story is of the Virtues subduing the Deadly Sins, which is called the Psychomachia. The Virtues are almost always female Knights Errant, wearing tunics over their chain mail, nonchalantly leaning on the spears that transpierce the imps at their feet. The Lady Knights are calm, the little imps struggle, curse, agonize. If the portal called for even more rings of carving, there remained the Labours of the Months, the Signs of the Zodiac, even satirical figures borrowed from fables or the books called 'Bestiaries'.

Pattern is the key to them all. It was not till the Gothic age that the statuary became fully humanized. These delicate Poitevin carvings must be regarded primarily as adornment of the churches. The small size of each detail, the complex relief, which is not bas-relief, but deep-graven intricacy, render it easy to stop at the decorative effect. But this is to miss three-quarters of the significance of the carvings. There is the pleasure of the eye; there is the enquiry into the subject; there is the endless symbolism. For everything in the Middle Ages was weighted by a double meaning, by allegory. The birds facing each other may symbolize eternity, but what do the harpies mean? Not, it is possible, much even in their own time. Faith was a tricky thing; it behoved artists to be cautious, lest some authority should call them heretical. The same limitation was applied to the scriptural scenes. They were carefully selected. The church walls might be the Bible of the people, but the Bible is an explosive collection of books, packed to the covers with dangerous thoughts. To read it was the privilege of the clergy, if they knew enough Latin. It was forbidden to the laity; and how many of the laity could read? For instance if an abbot building an abbey had had the Commandments read during supper to his monks, what would have become of his carved church? For the Second Commandment totally forbids graven images. The answer is that the text of the Commandments was not pressed upon the monks. Thus the churches afford an extremely interesting study of the eleventh-century version of the Christian religion, as it was taught to the congregation of the faithful.

A close observer will notice an odd thing about the carvings. The faces of the saints or of the Britomart Virtues are purely stylized; the characters are without individuality. But here and there is a real, human face among the carvings. Under the curl of a cabbage-leaf peeps out a tiny head, smiling sometimes, more often gravely attentive. The first few I noticed I imagined were devils, or images of the Sylvan Pan, similar to the Green Man who is so often found in English churches. Then I became convinced that this was the work, perhaps, of one man with a natural genius for portraiture. It was none of his business to carve human beings as he saw them; but since all of his mates knew that he could reproduce them exactly, they connived at his game and sat for their busts. After all, if the foreman should notice and ask what the devil he was at, he could say, 'Why! The Devil, just like you say. He is lurking behind the leaves.' The foreman would observe dryly 'It is remarkable that the Devil wears the features of Jacques the Mason,' and let it go. After all, he was a master-mason himself. Only a generation separated these Aquitanian carvers from the new school of the Gothic art of the Île de France, where the figures were elongated and mystical, as at Chartres, but would soon develop into entirely naturalistic sculpture.

There is one exception to the rule of small-scale carving. This is a statue often found above a portal. It is a horseman, about two-thirds lifesize, and is usually called 'le Cavalier', sometimes 'Constantin-Cavalier'. It is supposed that it was based upon a memory of the equestrian statue of Marcus Aurelius that stands on the Capitol at Rome; for long he was thought to be Constantine.

Churches and Church-Building

Alas! French statues are apt to be defaced and broken. An angry mob delights in breaking the fingers and noses of human figures, and the slender legs of horses are even more brittle. I illustrate the Horseman of Parthenay-le-Vieux, because he is not damaged except by weather. The seigneurs of Parthenay once had an Archbishop of Bordeaux in their family, and thereafter called themselves 'Archevêque'. They caused their Horseman to wear a mitre and also to carry a falcon on his wrist—very odd.

Close study of the Aquitanian school of architecture seems to me to give conclusive evidence that it was derived from the East. The Oriental monsters and palm-trees suffice by themselves. Even after the split between the eastern and the western churches the habit of pilgrimage to the Holy Land continued. Pilgrims must have seen Palestine, and the churches of Antioch, perhaps even Byzantium or Alexandria on their long journeys. Unless we must consider the carvings as miraculously inspired, they must have brought home drawings.

There is one thing which seems to bear out the influence of Oriental art in an especially marked way. That is the 'Saracen' door. Many churches both in the Poitevin region and outside it, have doors carved in scallops, sometimes only at the outer edges, sometimes right through the concentred arches of the portals. It may be because they were simpler to carve in hard stone that they are more noticeable when the limestone gives way to granite as building material in the Limousin. But they do have a look of the Mosque, certainly.

There are other religious buildings in this region, such as the *Lanternes des Morts*, and the *Croix Hosannières*. The Lanterns of the Dead are little towers, with a chamber at the foot where the corpse awaited burial, and a windowed opening at the top where a lamp was left burning. This was a way of 'Waking' the dead. The custom was no stranger than that still used in parts of the Balkans in living memory, of leaving food and a light outside a grave after the body was buried, to appease ghouls and prevent them from digging up the body and possessing it as a vampire. The French built lanterns of the dead till the eighteenth century, but most of them are much earlier than that. The tall Hosanna

54

Crosses stand in the churchyard or in the village *place*. On Palm Sunday every year the people gathered round the cross, sang hymns, and made procession round the village. Some poorer churches have wooden crosses; you may see them laid along the wall inside the church on their sides. One savant told me that he had heard of a priest who had sawn off the end of his cross, because it was awkwardly long to carry. 'What can they teach these priests in their seminaries?' said he, bursting with rage. Not much about the aesthetics of church history, one thinks sadly, looking at the poor quality of modern *décor*.

4. HILL-COUNTRY CHURCHES

Aquitaine contains regions of hard stone, where the churches are not carved, or not much. They are much darker in colour than those of the plains. In the Limousin, and the Gatine, the granitic hilly country of the Vendée, the builders often tried to carve them, but the hard granite or freestone turned the edge of their chisels, and the carvings are usually '*frustes*'. This is a splendid word meaning 'failed' either because the art was too primitive, or because the attempt had met frustration.

None the less, the builders of the hardstone country did not let their dour material defeat them. They adopted a different style. Whether their churches are large or small—and some are very large—they built with a simplicity suited to the country. They used big blocks of dressed stone, and concentrated on the dignity of high pillars, and especially of spires. These could be seen above the trees of the forest, and their bells could ring out through the mists, to summon the people to church. The further you get up the Limousin, the smaller become the village church spires, till they are just like witches' hats. The churches of the Limousin abbeys form a school of their own, deeply impressive because of their darkness and their strength. I know of only two places of the Gatine, west of Poitiers, where they have succeeded in carving the churches. They are at Vouvant and Foussais. I have wondered if their fine carvings were due to the patronage of the Lusignans, for they belonged to the domains of that romantic family.

5. LATER CHURCHES

Aquitaine felt less than most parts of France the great revolution of church building that set in with the Gothic age. The only Gothic cathedral of the first rank in Roman Aquitaine is the Cathedral of Bourges, and by the time it was built Berry belonged to the French kings. Within itself, there were so many churches that the need for more must have seemed unimportant. But after Eleanor of Aquitaine inherited the Duchy, shook off her marriage to Louis VII of France, and married Henry of Anjou in 1152, the Gothic of Anjou exercised an influence on Poitou; the cathedral of Poitiers witnesses it, and the Plantagenet cathedral of Bordeaux. The most beautiful cathedral of the Duchy, or so I think, is that of Poitiers. Eleanor and Henry began its building, and the east end, of their time, has the slender pointed arches, the tall pillars, the flat apse, which the French call 'Angevin' and we in England 'Early English'. It seems to me that the former is clearly the more correct title. The style came into England with the Angevin kings, and their subjects continued to build it there and in their French possessions till the reign of Edward I. There are other Gothic churches, the Cathedrals of Limoges, and of Bordeaux, the church of Niort, and others here and there, but they do not compare with those of the north-east of France.

There are a few Renaissance churches, built in the elaborate crocketed manner contemporary with the great age of château-building. It was not Italianate, but a late flowering of Gothic. The churches are usually chapels attached to the new châteaux, like that of Oiron, or Champigny-sur-Veude.

The Counter-Reformation did not build around here with much distinction, though many new orders, like that of the Jesuits, were founded at that period. The only 'Jesuit' church which I saw with admiration is that of Richelieu. There was however one builder, François Leduc called 'Toscane', who was employed in reconstructions, and who had an original grace of his own. The façade of the Cathedral of Luçon is charming, and reminiscent of the contemporary work of Christopher Wren.

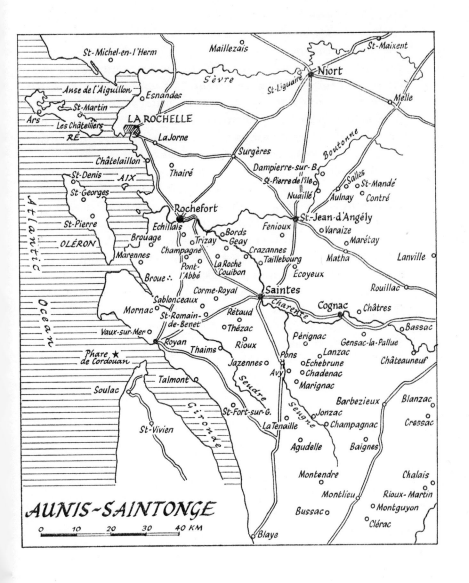

St-Michel-en-l'Herm
Maillezais
St-Maixent
Anse de l'Aiguillon
Esnandes
Sèvre
Niort
St-Martin
St-Liguaire
Melle
Ars
Les Châteliers
RÉ
LA ROCHELLE
La Jorne
Surgères
Boutonne
Châtelaillon
Thairé
Dampierre-sur-B.
St-Denis
AIX
St-Pierre de l'Île
Sailes
St-Mandé
St-Georges
Nuaillé
Aulnay
Contré
Rochefort
St-Pierre
Echillais
Fenioux
St-Jean-d'Angély
OLÉRON
Brouage
Trizay
Bords
Geay
Varaize
Marétay
Lanville
Marennes
Champagne
Crazannes
Taillebourg
Matha
Broue
Pont-
l'Abbé
La Roche
Couibon
Ecoyeux
Rouillac
Corme-Royal
Saintes
Atlantic
Sablonceaux
Charente
Cognac
Châtres
Mornac
St-Romain-
de-Benet
Rétaud
Bassac
Vaux-sur-Mer
Thézac
Pérignac
Gensac-la-Pallue
Ocean
Royan
Thaims
Rioux
Pons
Lanzac
Châteauneuf
Phare
de Cordouan
Jazennes
Avy
Echebrune
Chadenac
Soulac
Talmont
Marignac
Seudre
Barbezieux
Blanzac
St-Vivien
Gironde
St-Fort-sur-G.
Jonzac
Cressac
La Tenaille
Champagnac
Seugne
Agudelle
Baignes
AUNIS-SAINTONGE
Montendre
Chalais
Montlieu
Rioux-Martin
0 10 20 30 40 KM
Bussac
Montguyon
Clérac
Blaye

The eighteenth century, and even more the nineteenth, marked the nadir of French church-building. The clergy of the eighteenth century seemed capable only of destroying old work which they considered barbarous. When they came to building, they perpetrated the most grisly errors, like the heavy balustrades of the clerestory passage of Poitiers cathedral, or some hideous work at Bordeaux. As to the nineteenth century, better say nothing at all. The builders could only imitate the work of better men. Piety, to my mind, is no excuse for bad art. There is one modern church in the region which merits study, Ste.-Marie of Royan.

If the reader of my book finds this chapter on churches too long, I beg him to forgive me. It seemed to me that it would be easier for him to take it at one gulp, as it were, than to be faced with small doses of numbers of churches in succession. The Centre of Advanced Studies in Mediaeval Civilization of the University of Poitiers has done me the great kindness to allow me to print the maps which they give to their students. These show the Romanesque churches—and they show nothing else. If the traveller uses them, they will enable him to save himself much bewildered wandering, and to visit the best groups of churches in one expedition for each group.

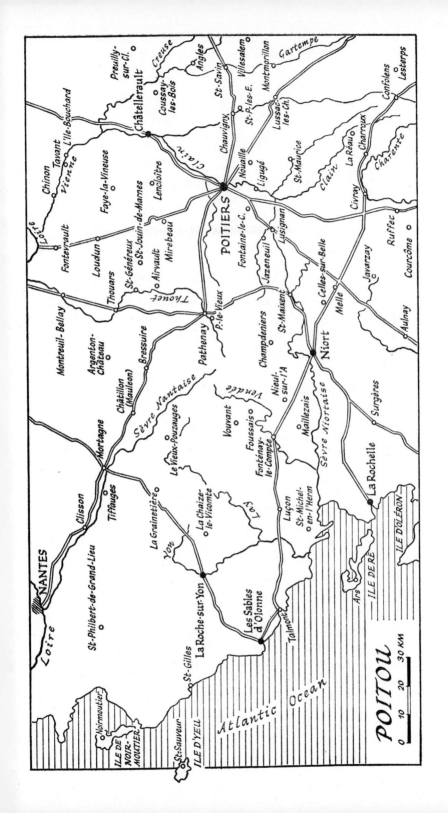

POITOU

Chapter Five

THE LOWER VIENNE

1. FONTREVAULT AND CHINON

Poitou is watered by several systems of rivers. The mistress of them all is the Vienne, a noble stream, beautiful through its long course. It rises high in the heart of the Limousin plateau, runs down slanting westwards through the valleys, and then turns north towards the Loire. I shall follow it here from the Loire upstream to Confolens, where it reaches the hill-country; and then describe its eastern affluents, the Creuse and the Gartempe.

When you drive up the Vienne from the Loire, you come at once to a region of famous places. A few miles from Montsoreau, in the forest, lies Fontrevault. This is one of the greatest mediaeval abbeys of France. It was founded at the end of the eleventh century by Robert d'Arbrissel, a Breton reforming prior. He designed it as a double abbey of nuns and monks, ordaining that its head should always be chosen from the nuns; 'The nuns should be over, the monks under.' This rule may have been due to reverence for the first abbess, Petronille de Chémillé, or perhaps to d'Arbrissel's recognition that women, properly trained, are better administrators than men. Trained—there is the crux; experience of many superiors, both men and women, has taught me that untrained women in power turn to tyrants, but that disciplined they are superb commanders; and surely the religious life must provide a thorough apprenticeship. The founder's trust was justified by the fact that Fontrevault flourished till the Revolution

60

of 1789. It had a period of decay, like almost all monastic orders, in the sixteenth century; but was reformed by two energetic abbesses. In the eighteenth century it was outstanding enough, as a school for young ladies, to be entrusted with the education of four of Louis XV's all too numerous daughters. When the guide informs the visitor that one of the abbesses was the sister of Madame de Montespan, he may be astonished, and more astonished when he learns that she was a devout and learned nun, the friend of Pascal and the Port-Royal contemplatives. The character of the Mortemart family shows only in the circumstance that she ruled the greatest nunnery of France. Françoise-Athénais de Mortemart might be a mistress, but she was the mistress of a king, and that king Louis XIV; Gabrielle de Mortemart might be a nun, but she was an abbess, and her abbey Fontrevault. Nothing but the best was good enough for a Mortemart.

The abbey buildings are better preserved than almost any in France, because it has been used as a prison since the Revolution. I remember seeing long ago a man being led under guard across a courtyard. He turned on the visitors a face so desperate and so wicked that I felt bitterly ashamed of being there. Nowadays there are still some prisoners, but the guide tells you that they grow steadily fewer, for when they are released they are not replaced. They are able to earn wages by helping with the restorations. Far more of the abbey is shown now than formerly.

There used to be seven buildings within the plain high walls: the convent of the nuns, and one for penitent harlots, the monasteries of the monks and of the lay-brothers, a hospital for lepers, another for aged monks and nuns, a guest-house and the abbess's lodging. There is a vast complex of halls and refectories connected by cloisters. An elaborate octagonal kitchen stands outside in a court. It has five fireplaces that could be used at once and twenty chimneys. It is like a huge beehive—the only other like it is the Abbot's Kitchen at Glastonbury.

The abbey church is most beautiful. It is a very tall Romanesque building, the lofty pillared walls sustaining a roof of domes, like the churches of Périgord. It contained the tomb-figures of four

Plantagenets, Henry II of England and his wife Eleanor of Aquitaine, Richard Coeur-de-Lion and Isabelle d'Angoulême, the wife
of John Lackland. The *'gisants'* are said to date from the end of the
twelfth century; they are naturalistic in the evolved manner of
Gothic art, and may be actually portraits—though hardly that of
Henry II. Eleanor is carved as an old woman, but retaining the
lines of her famous beauty. Richard Coeur-de-Lion, tall and dazz-
lingly handsome, is not the fearless and cruel warrior, but the
troubadour. The delicate features are sensitive, the mouth wistful.
It is the face of a visionary. Each time I am in the neighbourhood I
return to Fontrevault, drawn by that face, so like, and so unlike,
the tale of Richard Yea-and-Nay.

Fontrevault lay in the diocese of Poitiers in the Middle Ages but
the village itself belonged to the domains of Anjou. The most
notable Angevin place upstream is Chinon, which was a border
fortress of the Counts of Anjou, guarding the frontier with Blois,
a county usually allied with the Capet kings. Henry II Plantagenet
built the strongest of the line of donjons that run along the crest of
the steep rise above the river-bank. The little old town is delightful, built in two parallel streets, one by the river—I have seen it
flooded in a wet spring, with the swollen water lapping the door-
sills. Both this street and the upper one have many houses of the
sixteenth century and earlier. There are two churches, rather
badly restored; the more interesting is St.-Maurice, built under
Henry II. But the great sight of Chinon is the castle, ruined and
over-restored though it is. You can pass along its line of towers
recalling many a tale; but two most of all. The first is of the death
of Henry II. He lay there sick and at bay, defeated by an alliance
of the French king with his rebellious sons, and deserted by all
of them save one who was a bastard and a priest. Then Louis of
France took care to inform him that his most dearly-loved son, the
sneaking John, had headed the list of his enemies. The old lion's
heart broke, and he died. The other great moment of Chinon was
that day in 1429 when Jeanne d'Arc was admitted to the great
hall where the Dauphin Charles stood surrounded by his courtiers,
bearing no sign of his rank. She kneeled to embrace his knees, and
said: 'Gentle Dauphin, I am called Jeanne the Maid. The King of

Heaven tells you by me that you shall be anointed and crowned in the town of Rheims.'

She recognized him, but we, remembering that day, wonder if he recognized her; if the meeting with greatness lit a light in that dark soul. I believe that it did. Charles was not a proud man, and only the proud are blind to the blaze of genius. At least, he gave her her chance. He was near to the end of his tether, holding precariously to a few provinces south of the Loire, about to lose Orleans, the ancestral Capet city. He was undermined by doubt of his claim to the throne, doubt sown by his spiteful mother Isabeau de Bavière, whose recognition of Henry V of England as heir to the French crown implied that Charles was base-born. From that moment when the king and the peasant-girl looked into each other's eyes, flowed the relief of Orleans, the victory of Patay; and even after the capture of Jeanne by the Burgundians, her sale to the English, her condemnation for heresy and witchcraft and her burning at the stake at Rouen the current of her faith still ran. It renewed the spirit of France and even the spirit of Charles himself, in his fight for Normandy and Paris. This, the beginning of the union of all France under the kings, is the greatest of all the tales of Chinon.

Of a different order of events was the birth of Rabelais at the farm of la Dévinière across the river.

2. RICHELIEU

There are some very ancient villages near the Vienne hereabouts, among them Cravant, where the church is partly tenth century, and Tavant, whose church has frescos as stylized as those of Picasso of the Cubist period. But the most interesting place is Richelieu, a few miles south of the river. This was the heritage of the great Cardinal, Arnaud du Plessis, who ruled France and Louis XIII by skill, terror, and determination. Richelieu is one of those characters in history who are unmistakably great, and almost entirely hateful. He turned the monarchy of France into absolute rule, by breaking the power of the nobles, by docking the rights of the Protestants under Henri IV's settlement, by subsidizing the

Protestants of Germany to prolong the Thirty Years' War against the Catholic Hapsburgs. Of many lives of him which I have read, only two of their authors like Richelieu. One was written by a Fascist who regarded him as a sort of patron saint of that evil creed, and the other was his own memoirs—whose authenticity has been questioned—as self-justificatory as those of any modern general.

However, there he was, a younger son in a poor estate, forced into the priesthood because his family could not afford to keep him in the army. It is ironic that when, as Bishop of Luçon, he represented the Church in the Estates General of 1614, he argued that the King should trust the clergy because they were disinterested. 'Celibate as they are, nothing remains to them save their souls, which oblige them in thinking in this world, in their service to their king and country, only of acquiring for ever, up there in Heaven, a glorious and an all-sufficing reward.' But having served the throne with ruthless efficiency, Richelieu died having possessed nine bishoprics, of which five were archbishoprics, two duchies, four abbacies, and a farm. '*Ferme*': that sounds so innocent to British ears; why should not a cardinal own a farm? But his farm was not a collection of fields to supply his household with milk; it was a farmership of taxes, of a whole region. From collecting the taxes, the farmer was supposed to make his living, in moderation. The portion deducted by Richelieu was unlikely to observe any limits of moderation. Thus was amassed the fortune with which he was enabled to build the Palais Royal in Paris, a far finer house than the king owned then, and, in his own country, the château and town of Richelieu.

It stands, almost as he built it, Richelieu's fortress-town, a chequer-board of beautiful seventeenth-century houses within its seven-gated wall and moat. You enter each house by a gateway in the street, leading to a courtyard and a pretty gabled house—a gentleman's house, destined for one of Richelieu's followers, for he kept a court and the private army of musketeers which he so strenuously denied to other nobles. The church is a fine example of the 'Jesuit' style, classical and well proportioned. Outside the tiny city lies the beautiful park of the château. It belongs to the

15. Ste.-Marie-la-Grande. Poitiers

16. Confolens. The Old Bridge

17. Civray. Portal

University of Paris, and you may picnic in the grounds. But of the château only some ruined stables remain; this was not one of the châteaux which the Revolution would spare. Vanished, like the Cardinal who had nobody to leave it to save a great-nephew.

It seems to me that dislike for the iron tyranny exercised by Cardinal Richelieu in the name of the king has left a bitter taste upon the tongue of France. None of the ordinary guidebooks has much to say in favour of his private *bastide*. 'Decayed'. they say. 'A failure; nobody wanted to live there after his death.' There was no point in it for aspiring courtiers, naturally; Paris was the only place for them. None the less, the delightful old houses are inhabited; the people from round about shop in the market. To anyone with a sense of history, or an interest in town-planning, Richelieu remains haunting, and beautiful, too.

It was at least his construction, in a land which bears so many scars of his destructions. They were all justified by his slogan of '*Raison d'État*' all the ruined castles, all the ruined town-walls, the judicial murders, the many dead on his side as well as on that of his opponents, the starved defenders of St.-Jean-d'Angely and of La Rochelle. He exacted obedience to the king. He left an enduring resentment of the King's government. His mark, the fallen walls, signifies the fallen independence of the nobility, the fallen liberties of the townsfolk, throughout France.

A few miles north of Richelieu, the sleepy little town of Champigny-sur-Veude had a castle of which the chapel remains. It has wonderful sixteenth-century windows. By that date stained glass had long passed the age when men made windows like oriental rugs, with their tiny blended panes. Those at Champigny are Renaissance pictures telling the story of the crusades of St. Louis. North again, and lonely among trees, is the castle of Rivau, a jumble of towers.

3. LOUDUN

West of Richelieu, on the road between the home of the Cardinal and his first bishopric of Luçon, is the town of Loudun. It is a strange place. The circular hill upon which it stands is topped by a tall tower, one of the many built by Fulke Nerra of Anjou. The bottom of the hill is encircled by the base of the old walls, of which one fortress-gate remains. Except for a narrow line of modern warehouses and petrol-stations, the whole inhabited town lies inside these walls. Indeed far inside, for the shrunken population does not occupy all of the ground. The tower is surrounded by neglected gardens. There are three old churches. One is very early Romanesque, but it is 'disaffected', that is, deconsecrated and put to secular use, as the meat-market. It is sad, even shocking, to see the fine pillared apse overhung by a sign *'Tripes'*. The central church of St.-Pierre-du-Marché was the church of the priest Garnier, the protagonist of the tragedy of Loudun. There is another church, St.-Hilaire-du-Martray, a Renaissance building raised to house the relics of some martyrs. This contains a picture of the Virgin and Child, which is something of an art mystery. Its painter is unknown; the texture of the paint is Flemish, of the school of Memling, as I think. Art historians despise clues given by resemblances; but the regular, somewhat inexpressive face of the Virgin may be seen any day on girls walking home from work in Bruges, and the Babe, standing to pat his Mother's face, is too slender to have been painted by an Italian. There is a shrine also, to commemorate a time when Saint Radegonde, lost in Loudun on a misty night, was guided across the town to her destination by a Woman in Blue, evidently the Virgin herself. Also, piquantly, there are portraits of the Duke of Maine, the son of Louis XIV and Madame de Montespan, and of his child-wife. He is portrayed as a dark-haired boy. But for the survival of the little great-grandson of Louis who became Louis XV, that boy would have claimed the throne of France, and a civil war would almost certainly have broken out. Louis XIV legitimized some of his bastards, but few of the French would have accepted the fruit of his sins as King of France.

It was the priest of St.-Pierre-du-Marché who gave Richelieu the chance to ruin Loudun. He was the innocent victim of fate, this Urbain Garnier. He was not a very creditable cleric, for he was a fashionable preacher, gay and loose-living. But his real crime was that he laughed at the self-made Minister; and when Richelieu ordered that the walls of Loudun should be razed, he resisted it. By an evil chance there was a young abbess of an Ursuline convent in the town. When her convent priest died, she asked the bishop to appoint Garnier as his successor. Garnier refused, on the ground that he was too busy. The abbess began to have strange fits; she danced and uttered blasphemies, calling upon many devils by their names. The ecclesiastical authorities were perturbed; they set a noted witchfinder to examine her. (The severity of the Counter-Reformation had caused an epidemic of witchcraft in France, just as the same severity of the Reformation caused the same outbreaks in Scotland and the American colonies.) When the witchfinder asked the abbess who it was that possessed her, she answered 'Garnier'. Here was Richelieu's opportunity. He had the luckless Garnier tried. Under the most extreme torture he asserted his innocence, saying that he had never even seen the abbess. But he was condemned for sorcery and burnt alive, in the market-place which the people still call 'la Place Garnier'.

This took place in 1634. The judicial crime left, it would seem, an irremediable curse on Loudun. One reads about it in French history-books, or in Aldous Huxley's *Devils of Loudun*, a carefully documented account, and feels that the decay of the town, its air of dark foreboding, dates from the horror. Yet strangely the people seem proud of it, for the tourist is urged to look at the market-place where Garnier burned.

My impression of Loudun was cheered by a charming encounter. The strait street from the Porte du Martray to the church was lined all up one side by plants in pots. Every balcony was wreathed with creepers. A little girl of about four years played in the street with a cradle filled with dilapidated rag dolls. I stopped to say 'Hallo!' to her, and then saw a little old woman through the open door behind her. 'Are you her grandmother?' I asked. 'Yes', she said proudly; 'and there are nine more like her!' 'Will you allow me to photograph her against your beautiful flowers?' 'Ah! by the time I have finished with them I shall have the whole of both sides adorned with my flowers,' said she. Alas! The light was bad and the photograph unsuccessful; but the sight of that ancient street beautified by that granny lifted some of the heavy sadness of Loudun from my heart.

4. CHÂTELLERAULT. CHAUVIGNY. CONFOLENS

The road southwards on the left bank of the Vienne to Châtellerault is agreeable and deeply rural. Châtellerault itself is an industrial town, but it bears few signs of manufacturing disfigurement. This is partly because its main industry, arms-making, is sealed away behind high walls in works which may not be visited. The smaller local factories of cutlery are situated a few miles away on the Clain, which runs into the Vienne here from Poitiers. The wide boulevard of the city has shops whose windows, filled with knives, would make any boy weep with desire. Between it and the river lies the old town, pleasant with narrow ancient streets. The magnificent bridge, the Pont Henri IV, spans it to a towered west end. As I parked my car at the hotel, the host welcomed me warmly, for its boot has a plaque '*Écosse*', which I have often found a passport to French goodwill. 'Do you know that we have a Scottish Duke?' he asked. 'Yes,' I replied. Indeed the Duke of Hamilton is also the Duke of Châtellerault, his French title dating from some service done by an ancestor in the days of the Auld Alliance. From Châtellerault one takes the right bank. It is beautiful; tiny villages are visible among farmlands, and across the river is the forest of Moulière. At Bonnes the castle of Touffou is so perfectly set on the river-bank that you will think that you have seen it before; and so you have, in a book of fairy-tales. There is a great donjon-tower, and a tall main building of the Renaissance. It is shown to tourists; the guide conducts them by way of the donjon, which contains a room rather feebly frescoed. Francis I is supposed to have spent a night in it once; but the beds of Francis I rival those of Elizabeth of England in number, though differing totally in respect of bed-fellows. Then you are led through a series of dark and dismal underground dungeons, and finally you emerge in a museum of the hunt. Those who share my abhorrence of deer-hunting will

find the rows of little roe-deer antlers pitiable, and most pitiable a
tiny stuffed fawn, 'a few hours old,' says the label. Thus while the
view of Touffou from the river or the park is superb, I cannot
honestly commend the visit of its interior.

Chauvigny is the middle town of three on a great road from
east to west: St.-Savin, Chauvigny, Poitiers. Indeed it is only
half an hour's drive from Poitiers; but as I am here describing the
Vienne, I shall leave the others to their natural situations. The
little town lies on the east bank, round a market-place with a
Romanesque church. Above it soars a ridge of rock, a natural
fortress crested with buildings. You pass from one to the other of
five ruined castles, looking down at the houses below, for this was
the eyrie of a great mediaeval family, the Harcourts. The spine
narrows to the east end, on which is built the church of St.-Pierre.
From outside it is a beautiful pure example of early Romanesque,
finely towered, with a round apse encircled by chapels. Within
it is tall and narrow; the magnificent pillars set closely opposite in
two lines that leave strait aisles and a passage round the altar.
The pillar-capitals of the apse are masterly, and the most terrible
in France. They are carved with monsters and demons, sinister
and sensual—the monsters are all vaguely female. Some are
historiés—storied—a winged fiend with a wild boar's head holds
out a bribe to a bishop; whose right hand repudiates it but whose
left hand stretches in the gesture of acceptance. Most horrible of
all, a dancer with one head and two bodies dances like a pendulum
between the devils that devour its hands. There are capitals of the
Christian redemption, too; but they are not nearly so well carved.
The Virgin is dazed by the Annunciation, and so are the Mages
kneeling before the Babe. It is as though the sculptor could scarcely
believe in the release from his visions of evil. Guilt and despair,
those are the feelings that Gofridus saw—for his name is inscribed
on a pillar. The shocked observer has at first a sense of horror that
the Christian religion could ever have taught such cruelty in the
name of Hell; and then, on reflection, thinks that this was not all
due to twelfth-century Christianity, but the agony of a sick soul
who was also a great artist. But once seen those carvings can
never be forgotten. After an interval of twenty years I recognized

every detail of that Thing wag-wagging on the capital, as one remembers the detail of a recurrent nightmare.

While I am about it I should say that at Civaux, further up-river, the carvings are said to be by Gofridus too. It is a queer place, containing a graveyard of Merovingian tombs; the rough sarcophagi lie on the ground and are propped against the graveyard wall.

Lussac-les-Châteaux is the next considerable place upstream; it is there that the main road from Poitiers to Limoges comes in. Three heavy towers are all that remain to mark the castles. Still running south there are summer resorts for bathing. Isle-Jourdain is pleasantly set at the end of a series of barrages of the wide stream; Availles-Limousin marks the boundaries of the old counties of Poitou and Limousin, St.-Germain-de-Confolens where a great ruined castle hangs above the river-bed is just below Confolens, an ancient town with a Romanesque church and a fine mediaeval bridge, where the little river Goire tumbles down into the Vienne like a Highland burn.

Now the Vienne above this point belongs to the Limousin proper; and I will desert it for the Creuse and the Gartempe, its tributaries on the eastern side.

Chapter Six

THE CREUSE AND THE GARTEMPE

1. THE CREUSE. AUBUSSON. AHUN. GUERET. CROZANT

I shall follow these rivers from their sources to their junctions with the Vienne. This is partly because I have found them more beautiful in this direction, having driven them both each way several times. But it is also because I think that the traveller, having taken the Vienne upstream, may naturally choose to follow another of the parallel rivers downstream.

The Creuse is the next river running parallel to the Indre to the westward. It rises in the Limousin, in a cleft of the Plateau de Millevaches. This is not, as you might suppose, the Plateau of a thousand Cows, but the Plateau of a Thousand Springs; a true name, for streams run from it in all directions. The Creuse runs swiftly to the north in a narrow glen; the roads of the uplands are set with avenues of splendid beeches. There is a small tilted town, Felletin, and then Aubusson.

The Creuse valley seems to me the perfect region for my favourite diversion of travel, for which I have the private name of 'walking through the centuries'. Often the passage of history can be traced in the same town. Indeed in large towns this is natural; one begins at an ancient core and passes to modern suburbs. But there are districts where a completely modernized village neighbours one whose air is immemorially old. The Creuse valley has examples of both sorts, strongly contrasted. Almost all travellers, I suppose, share this habit of observation; it enhances the pleasure

71

of touring beyond measure. The more one learns, the more the centuries become recognizable, till it seems impossible to mistake the difference between a twelfth and a thirteenth century church. Of course the appearance may be denied by the reality. The lord may have preferred an outdated way of building his castle; the abbot may have been before his time. Those mistakes, no doubt, are sent to teach us humility; yet with study one becomes pretty sure of the broad periods of history, even if dates overlap, and the centuries blur.

A strange experience has happened to me several times. I have stood on the top of a mountain, above the wind, in a total silence and calm, and watched clouds blowing across the slopes below, in layers varying in speed with the strength of the gale at different heights. Then I have thought, 'It is like this that we can sometimes see time. Perhaps the ages, in truth, happen simultaneously; at least one can imagine them moving together towards the present, though some of them are bright and some dark, and with a shift of wind they mass together.'

There is a danger in this delight in watching the passing of time. It is possible to concentrate so much on the tale of the past that the visible present is unseen. Professional historians are prone to this unbalance. The archaeologists who lead the contemporary fashion in research are the worst. Not only do they tend to disregard beauty which exists now, but they are willing to ruin it for the sake of slaking their passion for digging up the distant past. France has many examples of this idiocy.

Aubusson is a town where the past and the present are continuously joined. It lies in the ravine of the river, so steep that there is hardly room for more than one street on either side. The houses, many of them, date from the sixteenth or seventeenth century, with modern buildings set between them. Nearly all are the workrooms and warehouses of weaving.

Even in the dying Middle Ages, the people of Aubusson wove tapestries to mitigate the cold of castle walls. The kind called 'verdures', full of green trees and animals, date from the Renaissance. The Revocation of the Edict of Nantes drove most of the workers overseas, for throughout France many of the skilled weavers were Protestant. But one of the great Intendants, the royal governors of the eighteenth century, revived the industry, and a school of design grew up which gave the tapestries and carpets world-wide fame. I remember a London tea-party where the guests sat on chairs reverently set outside the Aubusson carpet, with its graceful faded garlands and borders of flowers in the Rococo taste. The arrangement was not conducive to general conversation, and set me wondering if the old salons of Paris were like this, with the hostess throwing a sentence to her guests in turn, so that each could utter his premeditated aphorism.

Aubusson now weaves hangings and carpets. The panels of tapestry are still handwoven. They are usually reproductions of old designs, often charming. The same cannot be said of the modern designs, where flowers and animals are all too faithfully portrayed. The Alsatian is a noble dog; a tapestry Alsatian is awful. There are some of the modernistic school founded by Lurçat at St.-Céré, whose stylized design and bright reds and orange are more to the contemporary taste.

The Creuse itself is the truly timeless link between the places on its banks. Here at Aubusson, and right down to near Argenton, it flows in the Limousin and the Marche, through a bed of the old granitic rocks of the earliest hills of France. These crystalline rocks are impermeable to water, so that they can be dammed to form reservoirs for electric works. Not so the soft rock of the limestone plateau, where water seeps through the stone, down to the ancient sea-bed.

From Aubusson the Creuse runs in a gorge with the road high on the left-side bank. But at Ahun, a village with an old church, a road slopes downhill to the river and the hamlet of Moûtier-d'-Ahun. There stand the ruins of the abbey, the *moûtier*, as the South calls a monastery. Of the nave only the gate remains. In the choir, which is the parish church now, there are famous seventeenth-century carvings. They are made in the high relief of the period, in bog-oak, almost black. There is an extraordinary tangle of beasts, heraldry, hounds, mermaids, framing medallions of Christ and the Virgin. To my eyes the workmanship seems excellent, the design far too lavish. But an old man of Ahun who spoke to me on the mediaeval bridge over the river said, 'They are the finest carvings in the whole world.' My mind flew to Grinling Gibbons, whose carvings are of about the same period, and far better. But of course I checked this thought and agreed enthusiastically with that citizen of Ahun.

Gueret, halfway down the Limousin slope, is the cross-roads for all the province of the Marche, of which it was formerly the capital. It is an ancient city but its age is entirely masked by modern commerce; a vast market-place serves that commerce, which is in cattle. Except on market-day the *place* serves as a car-park. There is a good museum housed in an eighteenth-century hotel, holding a collection of old pottery and especially some fine Limoges enamels. Gueret shows the new life brought to the French countryside by the advent of the motor. Formerly the farmer and his wife drove their cart to market laden with fowls and vegetables to sell. Now they cram in the children in holiday-time, and l'Oncle Jacques, and la Cousine Mathilde, not to mention their neighbour la Veuve Billon. All smartly dressed in their best, they dispose of their merchandise, and then swell the pre-lunch crowd, and contribute to the vivacity of Gueret. I do not seek to disguise my liking for this modern hill-town, which has the advantage of being so important a road-centre that one comes into it often, on the way to other places. Once I took the beautiful upland road that joins it to Limoges, and was signalled at the outskirts of a village by two young men, for a hitch-hike, or as the French say, *auto-stop*. They were metal-workers, they told me, on their way to Limoges for their holiday. They could not have been more polite, but we passed an almost silent drive, for they spoke so broad a *patois* that I could hardly understand anything they said. Their strangely accented tongue was not the Langue-d'Oc of the Midi, but it was not northern French either; of course, I thought, Gueret lies to the south of the old language-frontier.

Gueret is still in the granite country of the Limousin. The Creuse runs in ravines till it is joined by the Petite Creuse, wriggling down from Boussac, at the artists' village of Fresselines. Then it reaches the barrages of Éguzon, where an artificial lake, the Lake of Chambon, submerges an old village. Now, hydroelectric barrages are admired by some, and hated by others who include me; but they certainly are the pure realization of modern French building. Just above the barrage-lake of Chambon a road runs down to the river-gorge where stands one of the purest examples of the building of the Middle Ages, the Castle of Crozant. It tops a promontory high above a bend of the river. It was a fortress of the *comtes* of the Marche. The ridge is so narrow that one picks one's way with care along a path from the square tower of its crest to three more round towers. Precipices plunge down on either hand; from rocky crevices old thorn-trees struggle. The line of towers must have been impregnable, when they were built in the thirteenth century before the advent of guns—and for long enough after; for a river-loop, if the enemy had no artillery, was a sure defence. There are many examples of this sort of building hereabouts; but Crozant, rising above the river with only a few small houses by the road, is the most solitary and the most dream-like of them all.

The traveller must take care to drive on the right side of the river from this point to Argenton. The west side of the road, high on a featureless plateau, is dull. The east side has various little roads by which one can run down to splendid views of the gorge. One is at Gargilesse, a village where George Sand had a little house to which she escaped from her too-visited château at Nohant. It has an artists' inn, and a delicious group of church, eighteenth-century château, and mediaeval castle, all tiny. The old church has some good carving inside, and outside a bust in relief that enchanted me, of a mustachio'd seigneur in his casque, with a face of such fatuous aristocracy that I felt certain that on seeing it he felt inclined to cut off the sculptor's head. (For mirrors had probably never come his way.) Then he saw the joke and let the portrait be. This fantasy assumes that the owners of silly faces are not always so silly as they look.

2. ARGENTON. FONTGOMBAULT. LA ROCHE-POSAY

Argenton, where the Creuse has emerged from the granite of

the hills to the limestone of the Plateau of Poitou, is an old town with some pretty houses by the river. But it is disfigured by one of those gigantic gilded Virgins dominating its skyline. The piety of the nineteenth century, deluded by the commercialism of its religious sculpture, led to the erection of those lamentable statues here and there throughout France. There is an interesting Romanesque church up the hill at St.-Michel, which partly atones for this. A very pretty road runs up the valley of the Bouzanne, set with castles.

Near Argenton, the Creuse turns west, and is neighboured for miles along its northern side by the Brenne. This is a series of swamps and shallow lakes, that makes a natural borderland between Poitou and Berry. At the west end of the Brenne, where the Creuse bends north-west, is le Blanc, a growing industrial town, fiendish to drive through, since its crammed market is unavoidable. But having recovered from this ordeal, you see from the river road the Abbey of Fontgombault.

Fontgombault is one of the most beautiful abbeys still inhabited by monks in all France. It was built at the height of the Romanesque style of Poitou. It is as large as a cathedral. It was deserted and the nave fell in ruins, then in the nineteenth century it was reoccupied by Trappist monks, who rebuilt the fallen west end. It is a great pleasure to record that this is one of the rare examples of wholly satisfying restoration. Nobody could mistake it for original Romanesque. But it preserves the style and is beautiful in itself. Inside the majestic nave runs to the transepts and choir, which are the ancient building. This I can state only at second hand, for of course, as a woman, I was debarred from entering the choir, and it is heavily screened. The west end has a wide courtyard, surrounded on three sides with various buildings. The present monks—they are not now Trappists—are craftsmen. They make pottery, a pleasant slipware of cream and dark grey over a red clay. The pottery shop has shelves of vessels, with its price marked on each, and a tin with a slit for payment; there is nobody there to sell. 'How delightful that the monks think it possible to trust the passerby!' I thought, taking an ashtray and leaving two francs. I wish now that I had bought more, but pottery is awkward

to carry by car. It is apt to quarrel with other luggage, and which-
ever wins, there is a stricken field. I have heard tell that during the
last war Fontgombault lent shelter and a monk's robe to a member of the Resistance pursued by the Gestapo. The monks risked
torture and death. If the tale is true, they are not only holy men,
but generous and brave, too.

Below le Blanc where the main road turns off towards St.-Savin
and eventually Poitiers, the Creuse valley is quiet and drowsy. Its
left bank lies close under cliffs; the right rolls away in fields. There
are occasional immemorial tiny villages up side roads on the right
bank. On the other side the peninsula between the Creuse and the
Gartempe is a narrowing forested plateau, repeated after the
Gartempe joins the Creuse by another triangle between the
Creuse and the Vienne. Almost opposite to Fontgombault lies
Angles-sur-Anglin, a tiny ancient burgh with a spectacular ruined
castle above the cliffs of the little river Anglin. A silent and deserted place. Haunted, I thought, for I was there at a season when
most of the people would be outside it in the fields. Further
downstream, just below the junction of the Creuse and the Gartempe, la Roche-Posay crowns the height. There is a charming
view from the bridge, then the street climbs to the plateau.
There is a spa whose medicinal waters are drunk by invalids,
and whose restaurants are frequented by masses of tourists on a
summer Sunday. The tourist had better not count on getting a
meal there unless he arrives well before noon, but the lovely view
down the Creuse valley compensates for hunger, perhaps.

From that point on, the roads are beautiful on both sides of the
river. It is set with hamlets and castles, sleepy and quiet, a land of
immemorial farming. Even the little town of Lahaye-Descartes
hardly interrupts that peace; though it is nice to think that its
double name is due to the birth of Descartes there. France often
names a street after a hero; but to add his name to a town is rare,
and denotes the honour in which the author of the *Discours sur la
Méthode* is held. Deservedly, for his thought dominated the reason-
ing of the French till it was rivalled by that of Newton; and it has
formed much of French mental training till today. A few kilometres on, the Creuse slides into the Vienne.

3. THE GARTEMPE. LE DORAT. VILLESALEM

The Gartempe rises in the hills near Gueret, and runs in secluded and sparsely inhabited glens towards the west. The tourist will probably take the road from Gueret to Bussière, which keeps the ridges and passes some interesting places. La Souterraine, Magnac-Laval, and le Dorat all have fine churches. La Souterraine slants uphill to a great gate and a Romanesque church, which has a beautiful tower and a 'Saracen' door. Two things annoyed me there; I could not see the Lanterne des Morts which is inaccessibly locked in the graveyard, and I asked in vain for an explanation of its name; for La Souterraine lies boldly on a hillside. I guessed that it is due to a miraculous well in the crypt of the church; but that is only a guess; so I drove away crossly to Magnac-Laval, where a roadside encounter restored my equanimity. A small procession was halted at a crossroads. It consisted of a farm-float decorated with wreaths of flowers and a poster 'Join Our Fête'. A brass band stood by, and a choir of children in home-made fancy dress, with paper crowns on their heads. A couple of cars were also stopped. I asked one of them, 'What fête is this?' The driver answered, 'Oh! Just the fête of the *commune*. It begins at dawn and goes round the crosses, and sings at each one.' Then I remembered that this was the Monday of Whitsun, and that on the Monday of Pentecost the people of Magnac-Laval hold the Fête of the Nine Leagues, beginning with a dawn Mass and visiting the forty-eight crosses of the *commune* bounds. They celebrate the return of their patron saint, St. Maximin, from Rome. I find no information about St. Maximin in reference-books except that he was a bishop of Treves, which seems to have little bearing on Magnac-Laval; but I think that a patron saint who is remembered by a thirty-mile walk every year for thirteen hundred years, must have been a lovable saint.

Greatly cheered, I drove on to le Dorat. The old town owes its name to its church, whose spire is topped by a gilded angel, 'le Dorat'. The town itself is delightful, with an old fortified gate, and streets lined with nunneries and schools, so many that it has the nickname of *la ville sainte*. But its holiness is really due to the church. It is Romanesque, built of blocks of reddish granite. The hard stone imposes a simplicity which throws all the emphasis upon harmony of construction. This is true of all Limousin churches, and although the experts call le Dorat 'mixed', because of some of its features due no doubt to the neighbourhood of Poitou, it is essentially Limousin, for in it the ideals of strength and simplicity are perfectly realized.

Legend says that it was originally one of the small missions planted in France in the days of the Irish saint Colomban; it used to be called St.-Pierre Scotorum; that is St.-Pierre of the Scots, as the Irish were called then. It never was an abbey, but was a collegiate church served by a college of canons, and famous as a centre of learning. The Abbot Israel was a wise and holy scholar; and when he was old he found in Théobald a disciple as brilliant as himself; between them they must have kept the light of learning shining, in that dark age, for about a century. They were both sainted. Then the Normans sacked and burned the church; and it was rebuilt in the early twelfth century, and endowed by a count of the Marche, to hold the relics of the saints. They are shown every seven years, amid great rejoicings.

In the troubles of the later Middle Ages an abbot fortified the church, but the walls and towers were almost all pulled down in a nineteenth-century restoration, so that the building now looks much as it must have done in the twelfth century. It is a long church with two towers. One is a massive belfry tower set at the west end, above a Saracen door. The other stands over the transept crossing; it is the glory of le Dorat. It is a slender octagon made of three lessening stories of round-headed arches before the spire tapers up to the gilded angel. The lowest row of pillars contains and illuminates the dome above the altar. This tower is simple enough, but to my mind it is the most beautiful of all the spires of the Limousin, a country of spires.

Inside the church fine proportion and lighting create a strong emotion. You enter through the west door and find yourself at the top of a broad stairway leading down to the nave. This device, common in churches built upon a slope, gives a remarkable view of the pillars of the aisles. The light is dim, save where the windows of a great dome set inside the transept tower shed beams of light upon the apse and altar. Some of the pillar-capitals are carved and there are old things, like a delightful pre-Romanesque font with two lean lions curled round it. The tombs of the two saints are plain and small; the relics are now enclosed in carved and gilded reliquaries.

The first time I went to le Dorat I was deeply moved, and wondered if I felt its atmosphere so strongly because it was dramatized by a spring storm which darkened the church, save where a break in the clouds poured silver light upon the tower and flashed in bars upon the altar within. But when I returned on a sunny day I was awestruck as ever. Save for Delphi, I have never felt a place so filled with godhead.

Le Dorat is only a few miles off the main road from Limoges to Poitiers. The small detour is richly repaid.

The principal place on the Gartempe itself is Montmorillon, a prosperous town with two things to see: a fine Romanesque church set on a terrace with a lovely view of the river, and frescos of Saint Catherine of Alexandria in its crypt; and a sepulchral chapel in the court of the seminary. It is octagonal, two-storied, and has some early and ugly carvings of the Deadly Sins outside. This is called the Octagone de Montmorillon.

From Montmorillon downstream the road is pleasant all the way to La-Roche-Posay, where the Gartempe joins the Creuse. But if the traveller has leisure enough, it is well worth while to explore the country between the Gartempe and the Creuse east of Montmorillon. It is scarcely changed since the days of the Old Régime except in the capital matter of land-tenure. The traces of the old days are there: the ruinous castles of the nobility; the churches with their domains. The agriculture is now, as it was then, pretty poor, it can never have supported a large population; the villages are tiny. One is inclined to think that the peasants were better off under the church, which had to look out for the subsistence of successive clergy, than under a seigneur, who might be dangling round the court at Versailles and demanding rents from a hard-mouthed agent. Latterly the whole region has specia-

18. Le Pont-St.-Jacques. Parthenay

19. The Castle. Chapel Thouars

20. Château of Oiron

lized in the rearing of young cattle for the meat-market. The majority of holdings are small, and can be managed by a family who are also the owners. It is a country of twisty lanes, where almost all the villages have either a Hosanna-Cross or a Lanterne des Morts as their hearts. I tried to photograph one such, but was foiled by the fact that it was the eve of the village fête, and the gypsies had wreathed the lantern with coloured electric bulbs, and left a swarthy youth to guard them against the village boys.

But the most haunting place in this whole region is Villesalem. The priory takes some finding, for it is not even in a village. For long it was used as outbuildings by a farm, and there are only a few cottages beside it. The tourist must mark la Trimouille, and then thread his way about the lanes.

Villesalem was a priory of the order of Fontrevault. The lovely ruinous chapel dates from the height of the Romanesque period. The nunnery was built in the seventeenth century right on to the west end of the church, connected by corridors broken through the façade. It is taller than the chapel, but far more dilapidated, for the seventeenth century built far less well than the twelfth. The Beaux Arts are reclaiming as much of the church as is possible. Volunteers are clearing the debris of centuries from the floor, and the delicately carved pillars of the nave and apse are almost entirely visible. The door-carvings are especially endearing. It is as though the builders said, 'This is a church for women; no demons here.'

The buildings are protected from wandering cattle by a wire fence. The guardian who admitted me had a face of clear-cut intellectual beauty; I surmised she was an archaeologist. I said to her, 'One can see what sort of woman that seventeenth-century Prioress was; a bossy woman; she had no hesitation in breaking through the carving of the façade for the convenience of her nuns. No doubt, like all the ruling class of the Great Century, she despised mediaeval building as barbarous,' 'Mademoiselle, vous brodez,' she said, 'you embroider.' 'Oui, je brode,' I agreed. And so I do. It seems to me that there is no harm in imagining the meaning of the past, so long as you keep clear in your mind that imagination is not fact, but simply what the old things suggest.

My encounters were not yet finished, for a man spoke to me in perfect English. He proved to be a professor of the University of Poitiers. He talked to the guardian of the clearing of the church, and to me of the carvings of the doors. Then he stamped his foot on the ground, and said with passion, 'When we get down to digging, there will certainly be something there.' 'Oh, Monsieur!' I cried in horror, 'you do not mean to excavate! You will spoil this lovely church!' 'We shall not spoil it,' he said. 'We shall make proper trenches, according to the scientific rules of archaeology.' 'But what do you expect to find?' I asked. 'Merovingian tombs. You will ruin the ambiance of Villesalem; look what they have done to Ligugé.' 'Mademoiselle, you are saying that my friend the Abbé, le Père de la Croix, has ruined Ligugé?' 'I am sorry if he is your friend, Monsieur, but he has spoilt it. With those ghastly corrugated iron roofs over the tombs, hiding the beautiful façade.' 'It is not spoilt!' he repeated. 'If you do it here, you will destroy the ambiance of Villesalem. You will make great coffin-shaped holes, and for what? Empty stone boxes; they are always empty, and they are hideous. For those you are willing to deface a Romanesque cathedral.' We parted in anger, and if ever I should see that professor again I should apologize for my ill manners; for one should not quarrel with one's hosts in a foreign land. But I have recorded this scene word for word, to explain the matter of the dispute that lies between historians today. French archaeologists are (as I think) mad about tombs of the Dark Ages. After their superficial conversion to Christianity, the Franks and other barbarians took to burying their chiefs in imitations of the sarcophagi of the Roman era. At first these were roughly carved; but as time went on and craftsmanship decayed this modest adornment ceased; and the later coffins have not even lids. They are always empty, save for an occasional scrap of material. For the acids of the damp that seeped through the edges of the covers, and the gnawing of the worm, have destroyed even the enduring bone. My only excuse for my dismayed outburst at Villesalem is that I had been much exposed to excavations during those travels, and had seen more than one ancient church disfigured. I could not feel that the robbing of tombs was justified by the absence of the corpses; for I thought that the Merovingians, like the Pharaohs, believed that their burial with holy rites in holy ground ensured their survival in Paradise. The old tomb-robbers were poor hungry Egyptians, seeking for jewels; the modern savants seek only for some tiny addition to knowledge.

Knowledge is fun, and the pleasure of the smallest memorial is lively. I look at a little flint knife, given to me by the great scholar of Périgord, Jean Secret—'I pick them up on the ground by the dozen,' he said. I cherish it, and reflect that I do not believe that a modern archaeologist is as skilful, or as good a servant of civilization, as the small patient workman of the Stone Age who chipped the flint to make that little, brittle blade.

4. ST.-SAVIN

Small lanes edged by watery ditches lead from Villesalem to St.-Savin; or the traveller may come by the *route nationale* that runs from le Blanc to Poitiers. In either case this is the right direction in which to approach the abbey, for from the east its tall spire is reflected in the still water of the Gartempe, spanned by an arched mediaeval bridge. So it must have looked for five centuries, ever since the monks added the Gothic spire to their Romanesque church.

The church stands in the town square dominated by the great porch bearing that slender spire. The building is simple, for it is early, dating from the eleventh century. The east end is rounded, the apse flanked by the round ends of the aisles. The transepts have a round chapel each, and five chapels ray out from the ambulatory passage that surrounds the apse. It is this structural simplicity that gives St.-Savin the ground for its interior ornament, for the porch, the roof, even the crypt are covered with the finest mediaeval paintings of France.

When you enter the church through the painted porch you confront two lines of pillars running to the transept arch, and then in a semicircle round the altar. In height, in placing, in proportion these pillars are incomparable. Their capitals are carved with interlaced stems and budding leaves. It is usual to concentrate on the frescos of this church, because of their rarity; but the nave alone would render it the summit of its kind.

The paintings are fascinating, and well shown. You must have binoculars. You can hire a radio apparatus; and a guide illuminates the roof and leads you round, so that your progress coincides with the script.

The entire barrel roof of the nave is painted with a double line of Biblical scenes, the dramas of the Old and New Testaments. The colours are faded, they are mainly in red, yellow and blue, but they are now aged to a prevailing russet and amber. They are not primitive, but drawn with sophisticated skill. The artist is a master of the expression of movement. The subjects of the panels are naturally serious in the main, but they are sometimes comic. The first thing the adorners of churches wanted to do was to edify the people, the last to bore them. God has never been represented in a more vivid way; He is frequently there directing the destiny of man, Himself a god made in man's image, the likeness of a father, of a great lord, moving with absolute authority and absolute kindness. He is distinguished from the mortals swarming about Him by His height, for He is about seven feet tall, and by His halo.

In the Old Testament, the story of Noah is comic; and so it is here. Noah, obedient but bewildered, packs the animals into the Ark, and when it grounds on a bare hillside God is there to receive him and the Noah family, with the gesture of the perfect host. 'Welcome to Ararat!' says the waving arm, as plain as paint.

The pictures in the crypt, of the lives of Saint Savin and his friend Saint Cyprien, are later in date, and brighter in colour because the darkness has preserved them. When you go out by the porch you find it painted with scenes from the Apocalypse in rather a slapdash way; it serves the purpose of the Last Judgments so often carved on the west ends of churches, and is meant to show the lay people, leaving the sacred building, what they may be expected to find at their end. The painter has read the Revelation of Saint John closely. There is a Virgin of the Apocalypse, framed in an oval mandorla, whom you might mistake for a Virgin Mary. Far otherwise, she is being approached by the Red Dragon, his snaky head trailing his bulging body after him. He wears exactly the face of a Parisian boulevardier (period: early Colette) surging up on the pavement to address a girl: 'Mademoiselle, will you do me the pleasure of dining with me?' The dragon's smile, blazing with lust and greed, makes just the same invitation, with a few words altered: 'Mademoiselle, will you do me the pleasure of permitting me to dine on you?' The virgin receives the proposal with the same calm and competence as her modern sister; she knows exactly how to deal with dragons.

There are two notes to add to this account of St.-Savin. The nineteenth-century restorers coloured the pillars; discreetly enough, but it is a pity. And somebody has touched up the dragon's head. He is obviously a brontosaur; now how did a twelfth-century artist know about brontosaurs?

Chapter Seven

THE UPPER VIENNE

1. LIMOUSIN

A la claire fontaine
M'en allant promener,
J'ai trouvé l'eau si belle
Que je m'y suis baigné.
> *Liu'ya longtemps que je t'aime,*
> *Jamais je ne t'oublierai.*

Like many people, I have no voice for singing, but an ear for song. My inner mind sings to me when I am tired with walking, when I drive alone. In the Limousin, it is always the same song that I hear, 'A la claire fontaine', one of the oldest, and to my mind the most lovely of all French folksongs.

The plateau of the Limousin has come often into my story, as the source of the tributaries of the Loire. The Upper Vienne runs right through most of it from east to west, so here I shall describe it as a whole.

The broad stretch of low ridges is rooted in the northern part of the Massif Central. The top never reaches to more than 3,000 feet, and it seems much less, because the main roads mount its sides by slow slopes. It has no peaks, only a series of rocky levels, from which scores of streams run away to the plains. Often enough, especially on its southern side, the summit ridge is surrounded by a drop of cliffs or steep grass-falls; this gives them the formation which in Scotland we should call 'craigs'. The

French hydroelectric engineers have had no difficulty in damming up the high plateaus to form reservoirs, using the beds of the streams as catchments, and barraging their lower ends with little damage to the scenery. The largest of these artificial lakes is the Lac de la Vassivière, which serves in summer as a *plage* for swimming and for sailing dinghies. The hills have their own names, but the Plateau de Millevaches is, to the people, simply 'La Montagne'. Its wide uplands hold the sources of many streams, besides that of the Vienne. Under its eastern side runs the valley of the Creuse, the principal north-south rift in the Limousin.

It is a land of granite and other hard volcanic rocks. Rocks and the flowers and trees that grow on granite. Bracken and fern, the yellow of patches of broom in the Spring; the purple of bell heather in June; the tiny vivid flowers that bloom on a peaty soil. The trees that persist even after clearing in a country that once was covered with unbroken forest. They survive in the hedgerows, in the deep clefts between the rocks where it is impossible to cultivate, by the roadsides. Oak and beech, birch and wild cherry; here and there the boring conifers of the Ministry of Waters and Forests. If the small farms cleared out of the forest were left to themselves, they would revert to forest in a matter of years. And, more than all, rain. The Limousin is the first high land that meets the wet clouds coming over on the west winds from the Atlantic; the Plateau de Millevaches has the highest rainfall in France.

The Limousin is not a department, but a region. Once long ago under the Romans it was governed from Limoges as a province. But it was too poor and too little peopled to maintain even its status as a viscounty of the Middle Ages. Richer viscounts from down in the valleys kept nibbling off parts of it; the Turennes from the south, the lords of Aubusson and the Marche from the north. The stable civilizing centres were the abbeys. Indeed the hard rocks, the poor harvests of this hill-country produced the claims of the Limousin to fame. And that was men; it was the 'land of saints', of Martial and Valerie and Israel. Also, during the Babylonish Captivity of the Popes of Avignon in the thirteenth century, of prelates. Three of the French Popes were men from the Limousin, and owing to the inevitable processes of nepotic hierarchy, a large number of Cardinals and bishops. The poets of the Limousin belonged to the age of the troubadours. In the twelfth and thirteenth centuries, a very high proportion of the troubadours found their way from the hills to the courts of the seigneurs where they could earn their bread by singing. But this happy reign of song ended with the annexation of Aquitaine by the French kings, as did that of the building of abbeys. The new lords came from the followers and kinsmen of the Franks; they were indifferent to the singers in the tongue of the south. The Capetian conquests, together with the vile Albigensian Crusade in the Languedoc, wiped out a civilization.

There remained the metals of a land of stone. Very early, the people of the Limousin, and especially of Limoges itself, were famous as metal workers. They made crosses, chalices, reliquaries, which were sought for from all France. The arts of Limoges enamel and repoussé-work are a very learned study, of which I know only the tiny amount that comes of looking at the treasures of churches and museums; so that I cannot speak of it. But the descendants of the metal-workers are the workmen of Limoges today.

The country used to be regarded by many French people as far too remote, and too rural to be well thought of. An army officer, checked in mid career by some fault or misfortune, was liable to be sent to the Limousin for the rest of a weary and unpromoted life; '*Limogé*' they said. In fact, there are large camps in the district, and walkers are apt to find their explorations blocked by the sign '*Champ de Tir*'. This forlorn condition is changed now, for what we all seek is peace and quiet; people retire to the Limousin. Even its peace is precarious; for they have recently discovered that the whole country is a reserve of uranium ore. Alas! the green land; better go to see it before it is too late.

2. RIVERSIDE PLACES

The Upper Vienne belongs wholly to the Limousin. South of Confolens its bed makes a great curve, turns eastward above Limoges, and climbs uphill to its source on the Plateau de Millevaches.

Historically the viscounty of Limousin reached its border at Availles-la-Limousine below Confolens, and between Availles and Limoges there are some interesting places. St.-Junien has a beautiful Romanesque church, which contains many fine things, such as the charming small statues of thirteenth-century saints—an enchanting childlike Saint Barbara holds her tower like a doll in her arms. The great treasure of the church is the tomb of Saint Junien, carved all over, and still holding the bones of the saint. They are 'exposed' every seven years amid great rejoicings. The Gothic bridge over the river has a chapel at its town end. An image of the Blessed Virgin was found there, and the chapel was built so that she may guard the crossing. She is so enveloped in draperies and jewels that you can hardly see her; but no doubt they were given in thanks for her miraculous mercies.

A short way downstream a side road leads off to Oradour-sur-Glâne. A notice by the roadside warns tourists that Oradour is not a place to visit for idle curiosity; it is a shrine. This was the village where the Germans committed their worst crime during their occupation of France. With the landing of the Western Allies in Normandy, the French Resistance rose and impeded the movements of German troops, wherever they could. The Germans in reply sent the Division Das Reich marching through the centre of France, massacring the people to terrorize the Resistance. This they did absolutely regardless of whether the people they killed had any connection with the resisters or not. At Oradour there was no question of opposition to the Germans; its destruction was simply the satisfaction of blood-lust. On the tenth of June 1944 German soldiers assembled all the men of the village in the *Place* and machine-gunned them. They ordered the women and children into the church. The children were led in their classes by the school-mistresses, the babies were carried in their mothers' arms. The Germans filled the church with poison gas, and when that did not prove quite effective, they machine-gunned the women, and then set the church on fire and burned the survivors alive. Then they searched the houses for the sick and infirm, killed them in their beds, sacked and burned the village, and went away. Five men survived under the heaped corpses in the market-place;

one refugee child ran away and hid in the bushes, one woman jumped out of a window of the church and lived. The dead numbered at least 1500 villagers and an unknown number of refugees from neighbouring villages.

The martyred village, its ruins fenced off, is now a shrine where pilgrims come to mourn and pray. They are not moved by the curiosity against which the notice warns them, but by the shame and penitence which we must all feel for the evil of which humanity is capable. Some years ago, a German youth movement made that pilgrimage to confess repentance, and was received by a youth movement of France, which gave a pledge of forgiveness. Forgiveness is a noble thing. For Christians it is due from the wronged to the wronger. Yet though Oradour may be forgiven, let it never be forgotten.

Rochechouart lies some miles away from the river to the west. It contains the château of that astonishing family, the Mortemart; in Madame de Montespan's day they called themselves the Rochechouart de Mortemart. The original Mortemart castle is hereabouts among the hills. Rochechouart castle is very grand, of the usual construction, four great towers and a Renaissance dwelling between them. It now is the Town Hall. The church has a modern spire of a witch's hat twisted like barley-sugar.

3. LIMOGES

Limoges is, as its name suggests, the capital of the old viscounty of the Limousin. It is set on the west bank of the Vienne; and the best view of it is from the river, where you look across two twelfth-century bridges to the town rising steeply up to a sky-line serried by two spires and a tall tower. The Limousin was always a poor country, with a small scattered population. In order to live the people have developed art and industry, and that is the reason for both old and new Limoges.

The Cathedral is Gothic, built over several centuries. Its tall tower has three octagonal stories topped by a square one; it has lost its spire. The north transept has a fine portal of the Flamboyant period. It seems to me to be rather a sad church, but I cannot tell why. The two other old churches are Gothic too, but St.-Pierre-de-Queyroux has been considerably restored. The most interesting church of Limoges is St.-Michel-des-Lions which has a brilliant spire like a lance and a great portal on the market. There is an excellent museum called the Musée Adrien-Dubouche, with collections of Limoges enamels and porcelains from many lands. The streets of the old town round those churches are amusing to wander in. The market is always packed with people seeking for 'seconds' of china or shoes, for those are the modern industries of Limoges.

The famous mediaeval metal-work of the town was of ecclesiastical inspiration, for it was chiefly crosses, reliquaries and other church ornaments. It had three phases; first of inlaid jewels, then of embossed work, last of coloured enamelling. Its sale must have been made mainly to pilgrims, for Limoges was at the crossroads of two of the great routes to Compostella. It is an odd thing, but it is still haunted by the tradition of the great Abbey of St.-Martial, which stood outside the town walls, and of which not a stone remains. Citizens of Limoges will always tell you about Saint Martial sooner or later. He was the apostle of Limoges, and his body was the relic pilgrims revered. The monks became famous for their art, which was that of design and illustration. They were constantly quarrelling with the town council, but none the less it must have been due to their influence that the metal-work became known through all the land. They were rich, and proud. They claimed that Saint Martial was one of the original twelve apostles; or at least, that he was one of the seventy-two who received the grace of Pentecost. Seeing he died about A.D. 250 this does not seem a likely story; but abbot after abbot badgered the Popes to declare that Saint Martial was in fact an apostle. At length they extracted this declaration out of one of the Avignon Popes, and it was even semi-confirmed, for the practice of Limoges only, by a Pope of the nineteenth century. Which seems to show that the mind of a commercial town was shared by its monks. However, the abbey decayed. In the indifferent days before the Reformation, it passed into lay ownership, when its last four monks removed to another monastery; and the relics of Saint Martial were consigned to the church of St.-Michel-des-Lions, where they are still. The king bought the library of manuscripts of the abbey, which now form one of the glories of the National Archives. I saw some of them in an exhibition at Limoges years ago; they were wonderful, especially those of the twelfth century. There was a very great designer among the monks, whose drawings for church carvings, with the sweep of drapery, the flight of double-jointed angels, are in the style of the School of Toulouse—as indeed is the tomb of St. Junien, and the sculpture of the west front of Angoulême cathedral.

A large amount of Limoges metal-work survives. It is usually fairly small, so that one supposes the priests were able to bury it in a secret place on the approach of the *routiers* of the Middle Ages, of the Huguenot iconoclasts of the Wars of Religion, and of the tax-collectors of the Revolution, eager to turn anything valuable into cash for a bankrupt government.

The history of Limoges china is far more recent. The royal intendants had replaced the monks as the encouragers of industry. They revived the making of pottery early in the eighteenth century, and of porcelain when a vein of kaolin clay was found at St. Yriex up in the hills. Later an impetus was given by an American called Haviland, who started export to the United States; there is still a Haviland factory in Limoges. Early Limoges is charming and very rare. Modern porcelain is still a handcraft. The town is full of china-shops, but the tiny tourist souvenirs are too loaded with gilt, and also very dear. If you want to get a simple but delightful set of china, such as the hotels use to serve their meals, you must go to a factory, choose your shape and pattern, and then it will be specially made for you. This craft is still recalcitrant to mass-production. Auguste Renoir served his apprenticeship as a china-painter of Paris; his family migrated there from Limoges; the *artisanat* of Limoges might produce another Renoir to-day.

The other industry of Limoges is a victim of mass-production. It is shoe-manufacture. The introduction here as in all western European countries of machine-made shoes has resulted in a monstrous over-production. The industry can only survive on the basis of making every man, and especially every woman, buy more shoes than they can possibly wear.

The nicest thing in Limoges is, surprisingly, the post-office. Post-offices, in France as in other republican countries, are rather grand, for they symbolize the State. But France, with one of those bursts of humane imagination that mark her civilization, allows each town to design its own post-office. The interior of Limoges post-office is frescoed. All the means of communication are represented as young women—the Telegrams, the Poste Restante, the Telephone, the Parcel Post; above all, naturally, Letters. And they are not those bosomy females who in the public art of former times adorned town halls and parks. Not at all; these girls are slim and agile, short-haired and short-skirted. This is not the prettiest post-office I know in France; my favourite is one which is so filled with indoor plants that it is difficult to reach the counter. French post-offices have another characteristic which the brutal English might well imitate. Britons expect their postal employees to contemplate hideous offices all their working lives; and their customers are forced to stand and write at wretched narrow shelves. In France every post-office has a strong table, and comfortable chairs, for the public who have to fill in government forms, and sit at ease to read them.

South of Limoges in the valley of the pretty river Briance is a group of places that make an agreeable afternoon's drive. The first is the Abbey of Solignac. This is a dark, wide, solemn building, roofed with domes in the Périgourdin manner. I know experts who find this the most impressive of all abbeys; but to me it is frightening. It was founded, long before this church was built, by Saint Éloi, the treasurer and goldsmith of King Dagobert who had the sobriquet of 'le Bon', because he was about the only Merovingian king who could be called good by anyone—or kind either. Saint Éloi founded the craft of metal-work in the Limousin.

Continuing on the Briance one reaches le Vigen, with a good Romanesque church, and a little further on, the Tours de Chalusset. Two castles are defended by the confluence of the Briance and the Ligoure; the landward side is protected by a deep fosse. You can scramble about this nest of robber barons; but the

Guide Bleu says 'beware of adders', '*prendre garde aux vipères*'. This is the snaky South, and for the Limousin it marks the boundary of this book.

4. THE HEART OF THE LIMOUSIN

Above Limoges the Vienne runs through gorges, with the road blasted out of the rock, and quarries in the cliffs. Then the Taurion comes in in its woody valley. Soon the road climbs uphill to St.-Léonard-de-Noblat. The small mediaeval town is tightly built round its abbey; one must park in the modern outskirts and penetrate the old streets, full of beautiful houses. The abbey church is Romanesque; it has been a good deal restored and is perhaps rather an architectural muddle. But it has two fine things. One is the tower. This is beautiful and complex. It stands on a huge porch, which bears three square stories surmounted by two octagonal ones, narrowing to the small spire. The windows of the upper square story are topped by slender gables. The other and the finest thing is the tomb of Saint Leonard. Not that it is an artistic tomb, though it bears the famous 'bolt' of Saint Leonard, which it is lucky to touch. But Saint Leonard, about whom the priest has an account on a sheet pinned to the wall, must have been truly a saint. He was a Frank and a friend of Clovis, so that he must have had the chance to be a conqueror under that dreadful king. He chose rather to become a religious, and finally sought peace here, in the forest, where nevertheless friends gathered to him. He had pity on prisoners, whom he worked to release; on the crippled and the sick; on women in hard travail, on the deer of the woods. His cult spread widely over western Europe; even as far as distant St. Andrews in Fife, where a tiny ruined chapel gave his name to my former school. The name of St.-Léonard-de-Noblat borne by the town here meant that nobody could enter his church without receiving the grace of spiritual nobility. Of all the Limousin saints, Saint Leonard seems to me the most worthy of reverence; for his example of gentleness in a cruel age, leaving a name to which the unhappy turned for love and compassion through the dark centuries.

The Heart of the Limousin

From St.-Léonard a main road runs over the hills to Bourganeuf, where a Turkish prince was kept prisoner during the Crusades in a tower called la Tour Zim-Zim, and eventually to Gueret. That is an agreeable road, but it is better to stick to the Vienne till Eymountiers, where *la Montagne*, as the people here call the Plateau de Millevaches, looms over the river-valley. It is easy to lose yourself, for there are many streams and many roads, but presently the signs begin to mark 'Meymac' or 'Millevaches'. The road is very beautiful, under avenues of oaks and great beeches. When I reached Lacelle, the ridge was cloaked in a cloud the colour of gun-metal. 'Storm,' I thought. 'There is no point in going into that cloud, where nothing will be visible but a downpour of rain.' I turned right and downhill to the pretty old village of Treignac, full of turreted houses. The downward road ran beside the Vézère, a river that is lovely all the way to its end in the Dordogne. I was brimmed with the pleasure of overrunning the boundaries I had set for my travels, if only by so little, and racked with desire to let my car go down; down by the castles and the caves, down by fairy-tale Uzerche, and little towered Martel, to the land of my delight. However I include this divagation in order to say to travellers that this col of the Limousin marks what I believe to be the most beautiful route from the North to the South of France. It lies by secondary roads, without too much traffic; it may be slower than the *routes nationales*, but it is far more pleasurable.

The next day was englobed in a bubble of rainbow light; the 'clear-shining after rain'. I retraced my way to Lacelle, and climbed the Montagne by Bugeat and St.-Merd-les-Oussines. From every rock beside the road sounded the trickle and lapse of water. Over one bog the road was carried by a causeway; a tiny stream was marked 'The Vézère' and within half a mile another 'The Vienne'. The villages crouched down into hollows to shelter from the winds. A farmer drove oxen to plough a field; oxen have almost vanished from a land where twenty years since they were so common. Millevaches village is a bleak hamlet where you pick up the main road from Meymac to Aubusson. A sign in the lefthand hedge says '*Source de la Vienne*'. You take the path across the field. A spring wells slowly up in a hollow of marsh-marigolds; it is the Vienne.

My inner voice sang to me:

> *Sous les feuilles d'un chêne,*
> *Je me suis fait sécher.*
> *Sur la plus haute branche*
> *Le rossignol chantait.*
> *Liu'ya longtemps que je t'aime,*
> *Jamais je ne t'oublierai.*

5. THIERRY AND CHARLEMAGNE

Off the ridge-road from St.-Léonard to Bourganeuf a lane runs down to the valley of the river Taurion. This river was a gift for the hydroelectric engineers. They only had to dam it and install sluices at either end of its gorge, and they had a reservoir some miles long, and a narrow steep-sided lake. It is bridged by the old river-bridge of Pont du Dognon, and above the water is a small new hotel called the Châlet du Lac. It is just such an hotel as I like, simple, spotless, where one eats good meals in the café. Above all, it is quiet at night, for the bedrooms open on a flowery terraced garden above the lake.

I was garaging my car when a little boy strolled across the road.

'Are you staying here?' he asked.

'Yes,' I said.

'Then will you go a walk with me?'

'Yes, when I have taken my case indoors.'

He was an exceedingly beautiful child. The face of a gay and intelligent angel, a head of silken dark curls, enormous shining dark eyes. We walked down to the bridge over the lake, engaged in civil conversation. He was called Thierry; he was four-and-a-half. He did not live here, but was spending the Easter holiday with his Dognon grandparents. His Versailles grandmother had brought him. He went to the École Maternelle at Versailles. Did I know any stories?

'Yes,' I said; it was impossible to say anything but 'Yes' to

96

21. Lichères. The Abbey in the Cabbage Field

22. Abbey of St. Hilaire, Melle

23. An old Chais

24. The Market, Poitiers

whatever Thierry might demand. I told him a story, and a fine story, about Saint Front and a dragon that he threw into the Dordogne river.

'Now do thou tell me a story.'

Thierry began a tale about how he met a dragon one day. 'He came out of a hedge. He resembled an *enormous* wasp.' His invention failed and suddenly he sang a wordless strain.

I jumped. I have never in my life heard so beautiful a boy's voice; sweet, high, dead true.

'Thou singest?'

'Yes, I sing a great deal. I will sing to thee after supper tonight.' I was delighted that he gave me the 'thou' of intimacy. We returned to the inn in the greatest amity.

We all ate supper in the café, the *hôtelier* and his wife, who was the cook and a very good one, the Versailles grandmother, Thierry, and me. The Versailles grandmother accounted for Thierry's dark slender beauty, I thought. When our meal was over, Thierry danced over to my table.

'I promised thee to sing.'

'Yes!' said both the grandmothers. 'Sing Charlemagne. Get thy disque.'

Thierry went off and returned with a sort of cardboard gramophone, such as I had not seen in Britain. He switched it on, and a steady woman's voice began to sing; the song was long and it served to keep the child singer in memory of the words. It was a cumulative song, like the House that Jack Built, all about Charlemagne and his wicked desire to educate the children of France. First verse reading, second verse writing, third verse reading, writing, ar-ith-mé-tique—'Ah! ce sacré, sacré, sacré Charlemagne, qui a voulu nous éduquer!' Thierry found it gloriously funny. His laughter kept breaking through the melody of that miraculous voice like the gurgle of a nightingale: he danced as he sang. His eyes flashed, the curled lashes fluttering like wings. We all laughed, till I had to wipe my own eyes; I was weeping with amusement and joy. Thierry returned to the table of his grandparents, put his head on his Versailles grandmother's shoulder and fell into deep sleep.

G   97

Now they told me that '*Le Jeu de Jeudi*', 'the Thursday Game', as the song is called, was sweeping the children of France that year. France has a great treasure of folksong, modern like this one, and old too. For a long time past it has been despised by a too urban schooling. Instead of the country songs, French children were offered the pretty frilly 'Bergerettes' of the Versailles court. Now, because of the modern fashion for folksongs, the old ones have been revived. But the best of them were kept alive, as the music of children's games.

Now I should like to remark in passing that the folksongs of France seem to me to have a much closer affinity with those of Scotland than with their English equivalents. One day, when I parked in a square, on which a village school opened, I found the girls were playing the game called in England 'Oranges and Lemons'. Two girls made an arch with their clasped hands, under which the others passed, till the arch came down and enclosed a victim, who was asked to choose between two words, by which she was bound to one or other of the leaders. But English children sing:

> '*Oranges and Lemons,*'
> *Say the bells of St. Clemens.*
> '*You owe me five farthings,*'
> *Say the bells of St. Martins.*

How like the English, mixing up the church bells with the bargaining of commerce!

But the French song is very different:

> '*Qu'est qui passe ici si tard?*
> *Compagnons de la Marjolaine.*
> *Qu'est qui passe ici si tard,*
> *Gai, gai, dessus le quai?*'
> *C'est le Chevalier du Guét,*
> *Compagnons de la Marjolaine,*
> *C'est le Chevalier du Guét,*
> '*Gai, gai, dessus le quai.*'
> *Who is it that passes here so late?*
> *Companions of the Marjolaine,*

Thierry and Charlemagne

'Who is it that passes here so late
Gay, gay, upon the quay?'
'It is the Knight of the Watch,
Companions of the Marjolaine,
It is the Knight of the Watch,
Gay, gay, upon the quay.'

Now Scottish children play exactly the same game, and their song is nearly akin to the French incantation, in its sense of danger and romance.

'See the robbers passing by, passing by, passing by,
See the robbers passing by, my fair Lady.'

Returning to Charlemagne, it is beyond imagination that English children should go mad over a song about how Alfred the Great wanted to educate them.

I feel it laid upon me to write a translation of my own favourite 'A la claire fontaine'. I do this reluctantly because true poetry is untranslatable. But the plain sense can be written

At the clear spring
When I was walking there,
I found the water so fair,
That I bathed therein.
It is a long time that I have loved thee,
Never shall I forget thee.

Under the leaves of an oak-tree
I wiped myself dry.
On the highest bough
The nightingale was singing.

Sing, nightingale, sing,
Thou who hast a gay heart,
Thou hast a heart to laugh,
For me, I have one to weep.
It is a long time that I have loved thee,
Never shall I forget thee.

The morning after the concert, Thierry and I kissed each other a fond goodbye. I drove away with my heart singing the refrain that seemed to me to express perfectly both Thierry and the Limousin:

> *Chante, rossignol, chante,*
> *Toi qui as le coeur gai,*
> *Tu as le coeur à rire,*
> *Moi je l'ai à pleurer.*
>> *Liu'ya longtemps que je t'aime,*
>> *Jamais je ne t'oublierai.*

Chapter Eight

POITOU

———◄►✦◄►———

1. THE PLAIN

Poitiers stands in the Plain of Poitou. That plain is a great expanse of limestone soil covering the former sea-bed of the Gulf of Aquitaine and the Basin of Paris, where the Strait of Poitou joined them at the narrowest point of the plain of today. It is about forty miles from east to west there, but to the north and south it spreads out far wider, to the chalky downs of the Loire and to the basin of the Charente. A wide ridge runs west from Poitiers almost to the sea. The plain is bounded by forest and hill-country on either side; but those regions must wait till they come into this tale at their own place.

The Plain is of great importance in the history of France, because it has always been the easiest route from North to South. Its porous limey soil absorbs and drains water, so that its surface is dry except when it is actually raining. It is cultivable; the peasants have a word for the earth, '*groie*', and it is closely cultivated. The problem is water, which is only to be got, apart from the river-beds, by digging wells that may be a hundred feet deep, down to the water-plane of impermeable rock. It has been inhabited by man as long as history is known; one of the first prehistoric engraved bones to be discovered was found in the cave of Chaffaud, on the southern slope of the Seuil de Poitou. The Neolithic Age left many standing-stones. Archaeologists dispute whether these marked temples or market-places; simple souls like me take it for granted that they served for both. The habit of holding festivals and fairs on the same day is common in France even now, for the arrangement makes both spiritual and economic sense. Every here and there the Touring-Club de France has set a sign by the roadside marked 'Menhir', pointing to a dolmen or a cromlech; tourists were much addicted to standing-stones before they took to visiting Merovingian tombs excavated by insatiable archaeologists. The most famous is the Pierre-Levée of Poitiers, where Rabelais made his students devour their feasts; but it is by no means the largest.

The standing-stones are among the things in which the Plaine de Poitou resembles Salisbury Plain. The natural formation is the same; the wide and desolate spaces breaking into beauty at the edges and in the river-valleys; the intimidating sense of ancient times.

A plain of old habitation, of old cultivation, of the passage of armies. The invaders came over the Seuil de Poitou, by the firm ground, avoiding the bogs and hills of the Limousin, and the jungle and rockfalls of the river-beds, which are to this day often unroaded. Besides, the junctions of the rivers provided natural fortresses, where the rulers of the people built their castles, of which the chief was Poitiers itself. No army marching either way could afford to leave that garrisoned place on its flank, with soldiers ready to emerge and cut off its rear. So the neighbourhood of Poitiers was a battleground for centuries. Some of the battles decided the fate of all France. There the army of Clovis drove the Visigoths to the Languedoc; there Charles Martel stayed the northward tide of Saracen invasion. There Jean le Bon, King of France, was defeated by the Plantagenet Duke of Aquitaine who was also King Edward III of England, in 1356.

The Plaine has innumerable roads, running across and parallel to the great *routes nationales*, to which they are infinitely preferable for the motorist. I have frequently driven for a whole day on these small ancient roads without meeting another car save a tractor or two. They are all tarmaced nowadays, though in some cases not very perfectly. As a result it is necessary to study the Michelin road-maps with great care; you may easily take a road which ends in a notice 'Chez Chauvin', and find yourself asking leave to turn in a farmyard.

The farming is mainly of livestock, especially of cattle, as it is through all Poitou. You may see the local cattle, lovely and stately with lyre-shaped horns, or the Charolais that are increasingly fashionable, with their heavy hind-quarters and common pug-nosed faces. Horses have nearly vanished. You may meet a mule, drawing a small cart with its canny stalking gait, stylized on its long legs—the mules of Parthenay are bred for height. There are many goats, especially in the more infertile areas; they are herded by shepherd-girls, and are beautifully coloured. They are exactly the same colour as deer, and look as innocent, till you meet their slanting satyr-eyes. Destructive they may be, but I know of no young animals so entrancing as the tiny kids, dark, leaping, joyous. The cheese made from goat milk is delicious; it is called 'Cabichau' and you should always choose it from the platter offered you for dessert. In the farmyards the ducks waddle to the pond— what a pity that my photograph could not include the noble dung-heap, as tall as the barn! The farmhouses are very plain structur-ally, as severe as any modern building, but redeemed by their many-tinted walls and red roofs.

The crops are naturally fodder, as a rule; beet, the colza with its bitter-yellow flowers, grass. In favoured places there are veg-etables and fruits, but they are not extensive except in the Marais de Poitou.

The Plaine is hardly beautiful; it is too austere. The traveller hardly ever has a long view; for the land rolls just enough to confine the horizon by slopes and hedges. The villages off the main roads are immemorially old; often they are enclosed within the lines of their crumbling mediaeval walls. The people are described in that excellent book of the Horizons de France, *Poitou*, as fiercely independent, devoted to democracy, anticlerical. They are developing cooperative marketing and field services pretty rapidly. Many of the ancient churches are ruinous or at best neglected. But the farm machines are new, brilliantly coloured and polished. I have never seen tractors so well cared for, and it was a spring of unusually heavy rainfall, deep in mud, that I spent exploring the Plaine. There was one tractor attachment, like a brilliant orange sphere of rings—a harrow, I think—as gay as a flower. One cannot but remember the long centuries when the peasants, even when they were freemen and not serfs, were economically enslaved by a system of tenure and taxation which made it impossible for them to leave the fields. Their families lived on the small surplus of grain left after the King's tax gatherers had taken poll-tax and salt-tax, after the seigneur had mulcted them of rent, after the curé had lifted the tithe. In bad seasons there was no surplus, and the peasants died of hunger. Children lay dead by the sides of the lanes, their mouths filled with grass. Indeed the officials reported at recurrent intervals that the country people were eating grass and fern-roots. Even after the Black Death of the fourteenth and fifteenth centuries had wiped out half the population, and men had gained some freedom because labour was so short, the life of the people was very hard; there were recurrent wars, when the '*Routiers*', the mercenary bands, as well as the armies of kings and lords, tore up the harvests and raped the women. This fearful oppression lasted very late. Vauban, the great engineer-architect, wrote an account of the state of the people and offered it to Louis XIV; 'If you saw them,' he said. 'You would be sorry for them.' And what did he get for that? Disgrace and exile from the court. Louis XIV was too busy being the Sun-King to want to look at the people.

The memory of those days, not so distant after all, lies below the surface of the minds of the peasants. I will tell here a conversation I had with the wife of a proprietor—a farmer owning his own land—which may serve as a pendant to my tale of the chambermaid who worshipped Queen Elizabeth. 'We admire you English,' said Madame. 'We think you are a just race. What we cannot understand is why you have a queen.' I meditated for an instant and then pointed out that our Queen was very economical, from a national point of view, since she costs half of the expense of the French President. 'Well,' said Madame, 'that may be true; but if we had the kings back, we should have the nobles on our backs, and they would take away our lands.' Her farm was on land that had once belonged to the Rochefoucaulds, I learned. But her point of view explained why the farming population, while it may be firmly reactionary in politics—and it seems that the farmers of the plain tend to progressive politics—is republican to a man. Also why these farmers feel but a faint approval of taxation, and since farming profits are most difficult to assess, are said to evade it. They remember those old days when a noble had only to show his '*Papiers*', his documents of nobility, to the royal officials, to be excused all taxation. It is they, the useful folk, who are privileged now. I must say I sympathize with this philosophy. All oppressive governments—the old monarchies, the modern tyrannies whether of the Right or of the Left—shear the country-people to their skins; yet they are not only the most useful, but the indispensable members of every nation; without their work we should all starve; beside them no bourgeois, no soldier, no artist, has the slightest importance. The peasantry of France have a sheltered position now; they earn it.

I remember sitting in a wood between Poitiers and Chauvigny wondering if this plain belonged to the North or to the South of France. Then I realized that I was looking at a glade of asphodel. Now that is the most legendary flower of the Mediterranean; if this country is not exactly part of the South, it is the gateway to the South.

2. POITIERS

Poitiers stands at the junction of two rivers, the Clain and the Boivre. They flow from the south-west towards the Vienne. They draw near to each other, part round a rocky promontory, and come together at the tip of the town. Both of them run in ravines, very steep on the outer sides and sometimes cliffs on the peninsula. The site is a natural fortress, almost impregnable, and a fortress Poitiers has been through its long history. It is also, as a good fortress may be, well hidden. For the banks of the rivers are about the same height as the rock of the town, and, as it happens, the chief buildings are not set on its summit, but down the eastern side; so that there is only a long stretch of houses on the sky-line. If you come by rail or road, the town is suddenly upon you without warning.

There are some modern suburbs on the outer sides of the rivers, but no true citizen of Poitiers would want to live anywhere but in the real city. Coming from outside, you cross one of the bridges. The riverside holds the railway, and a boulevard infested with lorries. Then the town rises up before you. The streets are very steep—some of them are stairways—and they are nearly all one-way. In fact Poitiers is a motorist's inferno. Far the wisest thing to do is scale the heights to the central Place du Maréchal Leclerc, find your hotel, park your car, and take to your feet.

These observations apply, equally, to the other Aquitanian towns, such as Limoges and Angoulême. I make them here once for all, because they must be said somewhere.

Poitiers, when you are on foot, is an enchanting city. It wears its history as naturally as a goddess wears her beauty. You are not directed to its famous places by notices; you just find them as you wander through the old streets. Kings have walked here, and princes built their palaces. Poitiers has the unmistakable air of a city which has once been a capital, even if that time was long ago. Even today some call it the 'Capital of Romanesque France'.

Of course, the Romans garrisoned it; there are the remains, very slight, of an immense arena near by. After the Romans, the Visigoths held it till Clovis drove them to the Midi. It was the capital of the greatest of all the great ladies of French history, Eleanor of Aquitaine, for Poitou was the personal domain of the Duke of Aquitaine. Eleanor gave her city its charter, and she and her Henri of Anjou began the Cathedral. Jeanne d'Arc was examined in the castle by a committee of bishops on her vocation, and by a committee of matrons for her virginity. Rabelais described the students revelling at the Pierre Levée, as today the students meet in cafés to exchange those endless conversations that are a major part of university education. Jean Calvin visited Poitiers and made many converts before he went to Geneva, and it was here that later the Protestants set up their synodial system.

All that is past, save the many churches, the palace of the Dukes, the University. Poitiers, the citizens will tell you, is a bourgeois city. It has little industry, it is not obviously rich. It is learned and proud.

Certainly the glory of Poitiers is its Romanesque churches. As you traverse it you find five major churches, and more that the guide-book disdains to mention. It was full of churches and orders of religion, so that the impact of Calvin was natural. For the Reformation was inspired by priests and monks. There are still orders in the town, and you often meet nuns. Yet the old religious divisions persist. I stopped a man in an empty street to ask him the way to the church of Montierneuf. 'Do you know, madame,' he said with a glare of fury, 'that there are forty churches in Poitiers? Forty!' I had happened upon an anticlerical; well, that too, I supposed. I do not believe in the number forty.

There are buildings even older than the Romanesque churches. I do not know if you can call a standing-stone a building, but the Pierre-Levée is on the other side of the Clain; it is a dolmen raised on stones, but three of them have collapsed. On the same side there is a strange cell called the Hypogée Martyrium in an old cemetery. Probably a hermit's cell, it bears Christian symbols as well as carved snakes that may be connected with the pre-Christian Celtic worship of snakes. In the heart of the town stands the Baptistère de St.-Jean, on an island in the street round which the traffic roars. It is built round a piscina of the fourth century; its main part dates from the sixth. It is a rough copy of a Roman temple, and is not beautiful; and houses a collection of Merovingian tombs, not beautiful either. These things make the Romanesque churches seem quite modern.

The most renowned of the Romanesque churches is Ste.-Marie-la-Grande, in the market-place. It dates from the reign of the Duchess Eleanor, when Poitiers was the capital of an empire stretching from the Tweed to the Pyrenees. Its west front is completely covered with carved work; the portal, the pillared friezes of the history of the family of the Virgin, of apostles and saints, flanked by two lovely little lantern-turrets with their pine-cone roofing. The storms of winter have worn the carvings away, they are really only distinguishable by the eye of faith and the directions of the guide-book. But the shape of the church under its obliterated ornament is complete and perfect. Ste.-Marie reminds me of an old actress, sitting to receive her guests in a dress of velvet with tattered lace at bosom and wrist. 'See!' she says, shaking out the spider-web rags, 'they are authentic. One cannot buy such lace nowadays. They are priceless.' But the visitor does not look at the worn finery, but at the essential beauty of the face beneath its wrinkles, at the classic line of the bone. Ste.-Marie has been partly spoilt inside, by the monuments of its parishioners, just as Westminster Abbey is partly spoilt; but it contains some interesting things.

The church of St.-Hilaire is, I think, more moving. It is older than Ste.-Marie, and simpler. Its interior is a forest of pillars, for it has three aisles on either side of the nave. It is silent, dim, peaceful. The history it has lived through was far from peaceful, like that of its patron saint, Saint Hilaire, who is also the patron of Poitiers. He was a brilliant controversialist of the fourth century, defending the orthodox doctrine of the Trinity against the Arians through all the breadth of Christendom. Heresy-hunters are the least endearing of the saints. I have found myself looking at a stained-glass window of bearded bishops, noting one with a sour countenance, and saying to myself 'There stands Saint Hilaire, shaking an admonitory forefinger in an Arian face!' It must have made Saint Hilaire turn in his grave when Poitiers became a chief place of the Visigoths. It is pleasanter to remember him as the converter of Saint Martin at his monastery of Ligugé, from which that violent missionary, himself a Panonian exlegionary, went forth to evangelize the valley of the Loire.

The other patron of Poitiers, Saint Radegonde, was very different. She was a Thuringian princess, a prisoner of war of the Frankish kings. Clotaire I married her, but it is to be supposed that she found the manners of a barbarian court with its rabble of soldiers and concubines intolerable, and she obtained leave from the Church to separate from her husband. She wandered across northern France from shrine to shrine, till she finished up at Poitiers, where she founded her own order of the Sainte Croix—the Holy Cross. There her nuns led a gentle life, with prayer and meditation, and gardens and fountains. With song too, for Radegonde had as her friend Fortunatus, a late-Latin poet. She seems, curiously, a modern figure, for we can well understand the friendship of the heart that lightens the life of many an educated woman.

Radegonde had more than her civilized mind and her order however; she is remembered for her holiness to this day. Her church,
built long after her death to hold her relics, has a beautiful Romanesque tower, partly masked by a Gothic façade. Her relics were
destroyed by Huguenot iconoclasts, but an annual pilgrimage is
made to her tomb, and those of two sainted successor-abbesses.
Saint Radegonde haunts Poitou. Every here and there one comes
on traces of her gentle spirit, like a clear small lamp shining against
the darkness of her time.

St.-Porchaire, in the main street, has a pillared tower that holds
the University bell. The other Romanesque church of Montierneuf
stands near the watersmeet of the rivers at the north end of the
town. It was built in 1076 by a Duke Guillaume of Aquitaine in
penitence for sacking the abbey of Luçon. It has a feature which I
shall describe here once for all. Montierneuf is a tall and spacious
building, with fine Romanesque pillars running from the nave to
encircle the altar. Now, the church does not have the altar set in
the curve of the east end of the pillars but in the middle of the
church, at the transept crossing. This placing is the expression of
the wish of many priests to bring the services of the church nearer
to the people. It is linked with the speaking of part of the rites in
the popular tongue instead of in Latin. Throughout this region it
is widespread. It is possible to sympathize with the motive of the
innovation without admiring its result. The altar is produced by
the ecclesiastical factories of church furniture in Paris. It is a
decent solid table of dark wood, pleasing when you see it for the
first time, and subsequently boring, as are all mass-products. In
some small churches it fits in quite well. In large ones it is aestheti-
cally inappropriate, for the oval of the chancel curves away behind
it empty and yawning. This is marked at Montierneuf; for the tall
semicircle of pillars seem robbed of all significance. They have
tried to mitigate this ugly arrangement by hanging a curtain of
unbleached calico along the base of the pillars, to mask their
emptiness; but naturally this draws the eye to it. The abbey is
quite different from outside, for a story of Gothic work was
added to the apse in the fourteenth century, and the church surrounded by flying buttresses.

St.-Pierre is to my thinking the finest cathedral in the region of this book, save Bourges. It was slow a-building. Begun under Eleanor of Aquitaine and her husband Henri of Anjou, it achieved its towers only in the last Gothic period. But this does not lessen its immensely impressive effect. From outside it seems like a huge fortress, so plain is its east end. But it is relieved by the flamboyant towers, and by the great portal of the façade—the vaults of the doors are filled with a multitude of tiny figures. The interior is a great rectangle, of a nave and almost equally tall aisles leading to a flat apse. This is the Angevin influence which came in with the Plantagenets to Southern France, and to England also, where it is usually called Early English. Those high aisles flood the whole church with light. The unforgettable treasure of the Cathedral is its thirteenth-century windows. Of these the Triumph of the Cross dates from 1212. It is a masterpiece, both in its tragic Christ, and in its marvellous scarlet colour.

After the churches one must see the castle. From the market-place, it shows its outer walls, with statues set on top of the buttresses, and the great donjon tower of Jean de Berry, which is called la Tour Maubergeon. In order to get into the castle, you have to enter through the law courts, opening on a little square where their classical entry hides the mediaeval castle. But once you are in the great inner hall, part Romanesque, part early Gothic, it is easy to see how a prince like Jean de Berry held his court. There is a vast Gothic fireplace, and a stone-work balcony under a window, where the statues of Charles VI, the brother of the Duke, and himself are carved together with their wives. The wicked Isabeau de Bavière, it must be admitted, is most seductive.

The old streets of Poitiers are delightful. On market-days those round the market-place are closed to motor traffic, so that the visitor can dawdle round the stalls in peace. The Rue de la Chaine runs up the spine of the rock from Montierneuf to the Palais de Justice. It is full of mediaeval and Renaissance houses. One is the Centre d'Études Supérieures de Civilisation Médiévale, where the outer walls are Renaissance, and the inner rooms are arranged for study. There is an extraordinary library of photographs of Romanesque churches, arranged so that the visitor can study them and save himself many a wasted trail. It is open all the year round. Its learned and kind directors have allowed me to publish the sketch-maps they give the students; they mark Romanesque churches, and nothing else, and are a great help in planning expeditions. Further up the street is the Hotel Fumé, a fine example of a great merchant's house of the sixteenth century; which houses the Faculty of Letters of the University. But everywhere in Poitiers, if you push a carriage-entrance open, you may find yourself looking at a grand house two or three centuries old.

The city museum is housed in the Town Hall in the central square. It has some good things, especially a first-century Roman Minerva, tall and straight, helmeted and bearing the Gorgon's head upon her breast. She wears a slight proud smile, and a slight intimidating frown. I fear the artists of the classical world never managed to love the goddess of wisdom; they made her look like the headmistress of a successful lycée. I prefer a tough little bronze athlete.

Here I shall make an observation that applies to all this region of Aquitaine. Two centuries of nationalist feeling have seriously distorted the French accounts of its history. They represent the three centuries of conflict between the Aquitanian dynasty of the Plantagenets and the French line of the Capets and Valois as though they were a struggle for national freedom. This they were not; they were a competition for control of the South-West of France between its natives and the centralizing power of the crown. From the year, 1152, when Eleanor of Aquitaine divorced Louis VII of France and married Henri of Anjou, till the victory of the Valois at Castillon on the Dordogne in 1453, the rivalry was constant; and fighting endemic. But under the feudal system the lords who commanded the man-power of the wars were faced with a choice that carried no moral imperative. The Frankish kings had the crown and were the overlords of all the seigneurs receiving their homage. The Dukes of Aquitaine, a much older line, were over-lords of all the Aquitanian nobility. The majority of French historians identify France with the Franks, they write 'we' of the incomers, and 'the enemy' of the Gallo-Romans. Some of the local guide-books say that Western France 'fell under the English in 1152'. Of course this is nonsense. I do not know what either Eleanor of Aquitaine or Henri d'Anjou would have done to a courtier who made such a remark; probably they would have had him executed. But no clerk or layman would have said it. England fell to Henri by inheritance from his Norman mother, and it was his task to restore order in a country which had decayed under his Norman cousin Stephen of Blois. But none of the Norman rulers of England called themselves English for centuries to come. Even the Black Prince of the thirteenth century spoke English only as a patois to talk with his archers. In the last stages of the Hundred Years, the feeling had grown into something more like nationalism, by the time of Jeanne d'Arc—though she was a Lorrainer and doubtfully French save by blood inheritance from the Franks of the barbarian invasions; Lorraine was not annexed to France till the mid eighteenth century. But the real question was, did the local lords (and their followers), prefer the duke to whom they had vowed homage, or the French king to whom the Duke had paid homage? Even after the final evacuation of the English army in 1453, Guyenne rose in rebellion in hope of the return of English rule; for Bordeaux was ruined by the loss of the English trade.

Of course this travesty of history does not affect the really great historians, except Michelet, whose romantic patriotism moved him to call Eleanor of Aquitaine '*la Vraie Mélusine*'. But the visitor to France had better read Froissart, to gain a true and lively account of the Hundred Years' War, at its height in the fourteenth century. He is veridical, for he knew the soldiers and their leaders, and revealed their motives, which were those of personal loyalties and interests. He describes the confused fighting with admirable clearness. He was neutral, being a Fleming; his standards were based upon men, not on nationality. He admires the Black Prince but admires du Guesclin, the great Breton mercenary, more. I am inclined by traditional sentiment to the Capet side, for I am a Scot. But I am not prepared to import the emotions of later ages into the tale of mediaeval France.

The glory of Poitiers was never to be the same after the death of Eleanor of Aquitaine, and the flight of John Lackland to

25. Aulnay
Church from
the East

26. Aulnay.
The Apse

27. Plassac
Church. West
Front

28. Plassac
Church. The
Tower

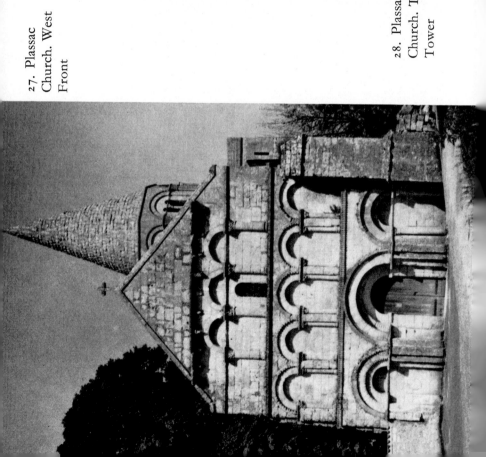

England in 1204. Her line had been the heart of the Romanesque civilization. Her grandfather, Guilhem VI, she herself, and her son Richard Coeur-de-Lion were troubadours. She held the last great Court of Love at Poitiers. She and her daughters by Louis VII carried some of the culture of the South to the glum court of Paris; the Countess Adela of Champagne was a marked civilizing influence. But the reign of the Duchess Eleanor, after she left Louis and married Henri of Anjou, was the sunset of the romantic glory. It must be remembered that till she died the county of Poitou was her property, and the Duchy of Aquitaine her realm. Her husbands might share the responsibility of government, but they were not the owners; only her child could inherit Aquitaine. That would not have annoyed the French King's council so much, if she had had a son by Louis; for there was nothing to prevent women from inheriting land in Aquitaine; but the certainty, so soon fulfilled, that she would remarry and have sons, meant that the French crown would have no hope of getting ahold of Aquitaine except by conquest. Meantime, Eleanor had Henri of Anjou, a great administrator and law-maker, to help her with her difficult dominions; and after he grew up, her third son Richard Coeur-de-Lion, her favourite, who if not a great administrator was a great general. The nobility of Aquitaine were notoriously unruly. They thought no better of the Frankish kings than of themselves; they had retained the feudal right of private war. They fought each other for a field, for a stream, for an inherited blood-feud. Henri II, even after he inherited the crown of England in 1154, spent most of his time in Aquitaine, till Richard was crowned Duke of Aquitaine at Limoges and acted as regent for Eleanor. He was fairly just, and extremely cruel. He fought the recalcitrant barons one by one, from his armed camp at Penne on the Lot.

Eleanor, by nature and inheritance, was far from incapable as a ruler. She gave Poitiers, and other towns, their bourgeois charters. Even in her old age, for she lived very long for a woman of that time, she occupied her retirement on the Île d'Oleron by organizing the laws of sea-trade; the Rôles of Oleron are the origin of all French sea-law. But she lived to see that great empire which she and Henri of Anjou had ruled together falling to pieces. Fundamentally, this was because it was too big and too divided; the threads of England, Normandy and Aquitaine could not be held by two pairs of hands. But there were personal reasons. The Duchess was herself a proud woman, but she married into a race of furies. The devil-ancestress of the Angevin line might be quite a talking-point; Richard Coeur-de-Lion was in the habit of excusing his rages by saying that they were all the fault of his fiendish granny; but the rages were fatal. The Angevins were always fighting among themselves. And Richard Coeur-de-Lion was obsessed by a longing to go on Crusade. In eleven years as king of England, he only visited it twice, for a total period of nine months; and what with his imprisonment by the Emperor of Germany, he was of little more use to Aquitaine. When he fell at last, in a sordid squabble about treasure-trove with a Limousin lord, the Angevin empire was doomed. His brother John Lackland was no match for Philippe Auguste of France, nor for the Norman barons who ruled England. In Aquitaine the French king conquered Poitou piece by piece. In the Languedoc he fell heir to the robberies of the vile Albigensian Crusade. The new seigneurs whom the Franks installed did not speak the Langue d'Oc; they did not want troubadours to sing to them in the old tongue. The southern civilization withered away. Aquitaine was destined to be fought over for centuries, and war does not favour art.

The process of decay was gradual, and had pauses. In Poitou and Berry the rule of Jean de Berry marked a sort of revival. Jean used Poitiers as a secondary capital, and built and adorned the great hall of the castle. When Paris was lost to Henry V of England Poitiers became the administrative centre of the government of the Dauphin Charles. But with the reconquest of Normandy this phase passed, and since then Poitiers has been the chief town of a province, no more.

None the less, Poitiers, once royal, then princely, still has the heritage of nobility. Queenly, kind, old with history, young with learning. A bourgeois city now, Poitiers is a splendid town.

3. EXPEDITIONS FROM POITIERS

Poitiers is the hub of a wheel of roads. An agreeable afternoon's drive takes the D.4 down the right bank of the Clain to Vayres, part mediaeval castle, part Renaissance dwelling-house. It has an enormous dovecot given by Anne of Austria to a former seigneur, as thanks for a night's hospitality. Even if the possession of a dovecot was the exclusive right of the nobility, one with more than 2600 nests is ridiculous. It is still in working order. Anne of Austria was ridiculous too, in the eyes of all women; men, of course, think she was a dear little thing. Further on is the château of Dissay, a white moated castle with a splendid fortified gateway. It was built by a bishop of Poitiers, one of the ubiquitous Amboise family. A shady drive through the Forest of Moulière brings one to Touffu on the Vienne and from there to Chauvigny.

The Clain upstream from Poitiers is secluded and quiet. Down in the valley is the ancient abbey of St.-Benoît, further south Ligugé, where Saint Hilaire founded the first monastery of Northern France, and where he received Saint Martin into the Church. A modern abbey is built on the site of the old one; it belongs to the Benedictine Order. Men can visit it and attend its services; on Sundays they are celebrated in the parish church which serves both the monks and the people of Ligugé, and are open to all. The church has a very pretty late Gothic front, but it is disfigured by the corrugated iron roofs erected by the Père de la Croix, who has excavates Merovingian tombs in front of the church.

Rabelais, when he got into trouble with the ecclesiastical authorities, was protected by the bishop of Maillezais, who was commendatory abbot of Ligugé, and lived in the village.

All this part of the Plaine is scattered with small villages like Gençay, where there is a church whose door is of the rather early period of Romanesque carving which I like the best; or Les Roches-Prémarie, where I have often spent a night at the Hôtel du Clos des Roches, because it is quiet and the cooking is good.

4. NORTH OF POITIERS. THE THOUET

North and north-west of Poitiers the Plaine gives way to the Gatine and the Vendée. All that land was once forest, and it still bears patches of woodland. Presently the granite hills of the Vendée give rise to three main rivers; the Thouet running due north to the Loire, the Sèvre-Nantaise north-west to Nantes, the Sèvre-Niortaise west to Niort.

The Thouet is a small gentle stream set with ancient places, and crossed by mediaeval bridges. It is easiest to follow it from Parthenay in the Gatine. Parthenay is a town devoted to commerce; its trade is in horses, mules and cattle. It is centred on an immense cattle-market. Part of its old walls remains, and it is famed for two things. Outside the town at Parthenay-le-Vieux, a fine Romanesque church is englobed in a farm. At the north end of the town, the Thouet is crossed by an arched bridge, with a great towered gate at the town side. The bridge is called le Pont St.-Jacques, and the street leading up to the centre of the city from the gate is the Vau St.-Jacques. For Parthenay was a station on one of the routes to Compostella, organized for pilgrimage by the monks of Cluny. At the bridge a company of pilgrims, with Compostella still so far away, could be admitted to spend the night in safety. One stands on the river-bank and sees just the scene that was so welcome to their eyes seven centuries ago.

The main road does not stay by the stream, so the traveller must diverge from it to look at the nice old castle of St.-Loup-sur-Thouet, and Airvault, with a Romanesque bridge and a very fine church.

When you regain the main road the town of Thouars stands superbly over the valley, a line of towers above the river-cliff. First above the bridge comes a vast seventeenth-century château, with a pretty Renaissance chapel on the road. The castle used to be the palace of the family of the Trimouille, great landowners of this neighbourhood south of the Loire, who were of that rank of nobility that came next below the seigneurs of the royal line. The château is a school now, and is not shown.

In the town itself, there are two Romanesque churches. St.-Médard, with a wonderful carved portal, shows that Saracen influence which turns up so oddly in France. The other, St.-Leon, is also Romanesque but has a Gothic chapel where the Princess Margaret of Scotland used to lie buried. She was the pledge of the Auld Alliance and her marriage to the Dauphin Louis, afterwards Louis XI, was as wretched as dynastic marriages usually are, and as a marriage with Louis was bound to be. As she lay dying, her lady said to her that she should cling to life. '*Fi de la vie! ne m'en parlez plus!*' 'Out on life! speak to me no more of it!' she said, and died.

In the plain east of Thouars there are two notable places. One is the abbey of St.-Jouin-de-Marnes. It is near Moncontour under whose tall donjon Coligny, the Protestant leader, was defeated by Henri de Valois, perhaps the best of Catharine de Medici's decadent brood of kings and queens. St.-Jouin stands on a scarp above the plain. It is a beautiful abbey, with a façade carved in the manner of Poitou, and arches of the tall Angevin kind; it is coloured a lovely cream, tinted with rose.

Oiron is nearer to Thouars. This is an immense château of the Renaissance and the seventeenth century. It stands in a bare plain, with a little river diverted to make a moat for it. One enters by a gate-pavilion, and is escorted by one of two colonnaded wings to the main building. The first floor is a succession of noble rooms, with immense fireplaces, painted roof-beams, frescoed walls, in the French classical convention. Why was this ostentatious palace built in this lonely country? The answer is that it was built by the Gouffier family, members of the new nobility of the reign of Francis I who made use of bourgeois ability to raise the money for his extravagant government. Oiron was merely a hunting-lodge of their still grander château of Bonnivet, destroyed in the Revolution. One can only wonder at the stupendous idea of a hunting-lodge held by Renaissance millionaires. A descendant was degraded, as usual for malversation of public funds, and Oiron was left as it is now. The Renaissance chapel holds the mutilated statues of some Gouffiers.

Their legend is more alive now than their history. For Oiron is the castle of the Marquis of Carabas and his Puss in Boots. One of the Gouffier titles was truly the comte of Caravas. Perrault's tale, if you read it attentively, appears as pure satire. Puss, bounding ahead in his seven-league boots to announce that his rich master is coming, represents just what the country thought of their jumped-up lords.

The Marquise de Montespan, after her breach with Louis XIV, was turned out of her Paris house with great enthusiasm by their son the Duke of Maine. She returned to her native country and took to good works. She had always been *dévote*. She lived at Oiron for a time, and made it into a home for orphans. One shudders to think of an orphan, housed in this palace and liable to meet Madame de Montespan in one of her rages, in its endless galleries.

The guardian's wife has made a brilliant flower-garden in the forecourt of the château. She must have the greenest thumb in all flower-loving Poitou; and it is all for love, for there is no market for flowers near to Oiron.

5. THE VENDÉE AND PAYS DE RETZ

West of the Gatine lies the Vendée, a land of little granite hills. Their ridges slant northwestwards toward the mouth of the Loire and Brittany. It is a land of Gauls, too. The Romans nearly wiped out the people of Armorica, Brittany, after a rebellion. It was afterwards repopulated by Britons fleeing from the Anglo-Saxon conquest of England, who gave their name to the country. But south of the Loire the original Armoricans persisted, and as soon as one begins to traverse their country one breathes Celtic air. Their rivers are the Sèvre-Nantaise running north, and the Vendée running south.

The Vendée stands in foreigners' minds for just one thing: the rising against the Revolutionary government in 1792. It was caused by a combination of grievances. The people of the Vendée, very poor, had expected that the lands taken from the émigré lords and the Church would be given to them. This did not happen, for the state sold the '*Bien publique*', and it was almost all bought by bourgeois from the cities. What finally moved the peasantry—for this was essentially a peasant revolt—was the persecution of the priest-hood. The Revolutionary government, with almost incredible folly, made the retention of their cures depend upon the priests signing an oath not to oppose the new régime. At least half the priests refused to sign; they were, in a country where the landlords were numerous and poor, identified with the old feudal Celtic society. The people rose and fought at first successfully, and then desperately, against the regular army of the Republic. They kept up a determined guerilla warfare in the woods and marshes, but in the end they were massacred. The memory of that civil war is still alive. The people are still poor, conservative in politics, and deeply Catholic in religion.

Napoleon, in order to hold the smouldering country down, transferred its provincial capital from Bressuire to La-Roche-sur-Yon, and made a network of military roads round it. La-Roche is extremely dull; and the people continued to use their old sunk lanes for travel.

I drove one sunny morning from Bressuire to Pouzauges. The hedges were untrimmed; honeysuckle dripped from its entanglement with a cherry-tree. I swerved violently to avoid running over a grass-snake wriggling across the road. Nobody had ever trained him in traffic-sense. Then I saw an owl standing on the tarmac, devouring his prey. I stopped. It was a horrific sight, for he was covered with blood. He glared at me with ferocious eyes, no doubt unseeing. But what was an owl doing, hunting in daylight, let alone choosing a tarmac road for his breakfast-table? 'That is a Celtic owl!' I said to myself. 'No sense of time. No sense whatever!' The cattle in the meadows were fat and happy-looking; that was Celtic too; Celts are feckless about human arrangements, but they are never careless about beasts.

The road led from Pouzauges to St.-Michel-Mont-Mercure, a tiny hamlet about nine hundred feet up, on a hilltop. A huge statue of Saint Michel is set on the church tower, and looks out over the treetops of the Bocage. Here the cat is fairly out of the bag. The ancient races revered 'groves and high places' as the Old Testament says. The Gauls did not run much to graven images; their charms are rare and crude; but no doubt they celebrated ceremonies on sacred heights. The Romans, always willing to adopt the local gods of the nations they conquered into their own Pantheon, more or less, built temples to Mercury on hilltops all over the Empire. The Christians, after the conversion of the Gauls, were instructed by their authorities, especially the Popes, to act in the same way. They converted Mercury into Saint Michael. There was after all a good deal of kinship between the archangel and the god. Both were divine messengers. Both were potent slayers of dragons, Michel leading the hosts of Heaven against Lucifer, Mercury aiding Perseus to slay the dragon and rescue Andromeda. It is however only in this Vendéen hilltop that the people have preserved both names: St.-Michel-Mont-Mercure, just to show there is no ill feeling.

There are few striking churches in the Vendée; the granite defeated the decorative intention of the builders, if they had any. Bressuire has a fine church tower, and there are two beautiful carved churches at Vouvant and Foussais. Vouvant has a remarkably elaborate north transept, on the chancel which is almost all that remains of its abbey. The little town is built in among the ramparts of the castle, of which the donjon is called la Tour Mélusine. Foussais is near by. Its Romanesque church has a west front carved in scenes from the New Testament; one of the ranks of panels is surmounted by an arch round which processes a line of cats. One imagines the sculptor saying, 'I am not well acquainted with lions; but I do know our cats. Better the cat I know than the lion I do not know.'

These churches lie at two edges of the Forest of Vouvant, a fine forest of oaks and chestnuts. It has a shrine of pilgrimage in a cave where Saint Louis Marie Grignion de Montfort retreated to ponder on his plan to convert the Protestants of the Vendée to the Catholic church. It is not much of a cave—granite does not lend itself to caves, it is more of a crack—but there are cafés below it to refresh the pilgrims.

Otherwise I shall confine my story of the Vendée to a drive I made one Sunday in June. It was very hot, and I had a headache. I took the road from Parthenay to Nantes, meaning to spend the night in the charming little town of Clisson. The huge ruined

castle there was the nest of the Clissons, a family almost as powerful as that of the Dukes of Brittany, with whom they were usually
at odds. Olivier de Clisson was the companion in arms of Bertrand
du Guesclin; they were both mercenary leaders fighting for the
kings of France against the armies of Edward III of England
Froissart makes no secret of the fact that he liked du Guesclin,
and disliked Clisson, who was renowned for his cruelty.

That road runs high above the Sèvre-Nantaise. At Châtillon-
sur-Sèvre I found a Sunday fair raging with noise. Fairs in France
are delightful, but modern advertising has rendered them hideous
with broadcasting. The *Forains* bully or cajole the town merchants
to pay for loudspeakers, which they festoon at every corner. They
then sell them records, screaming slogans such as '*Madame
Prévot, votre corsetière, la seule en ville!*' as though every woman within twelve miles did not know all about Madame Prévot the corsetière. Often the record does not even give a name, but just yells
'*Allez au Restaurant!*' The disk is so worn that its din is intolerable.
I fled from Châtillon to Mortagne, which has a castle and a big
church, stopped at the posting inn in the market-place and begged
for a quiet room.

Vain hope! Somebody was broadcasting here, too; jazz records,
one after another, with every note falsified by enormous magnifi-
cation. A vast voice cried, 'Listen to this little piece! I am sure
you will like it and join us!' I sat holding my head in my hands,
longing for it to stop. Finally, in despair, I went down and said to
the *hôtelière*, 'I am so sorry, but I cannot stay. I cannot bear that
noise!' 'Noise! What noise?' said she. 'That infernal noise of
radio.' 'It is not our fault.' 'I am sure it is not, Madame. You
would never do such a barbarous thing.' 'Well, you must blame the
Curé of Mortagne!' She was much and justly annoyed, but I was
desperate and departed.

Now this is, as I supposed, a manner of going out into the
highways and hedges to seek a congregation for the church. Perhaps the Curé of Mortagne succeeds in attracting people thus;
but not me. I drove back and dropped down into the river-valley
of the Sèvre to St. Laurent-sur-Sèvre, a small village from which
two tall church spires rose nearly half-way to the height of the

main road. There was a fishers' inn by the bridge, and I sank wearily to sleep in a room blessed with silence.

The loudspeaker of the *clocher* of Mortagne had done me a good turn after all. St. Laurent-sur-Sèvre holds the shrine of Saint Louis Marie Grignion de Montfort. The two tall churches are reproductions, as is obvious to the most inexpert eye. One is in the Romanesque style, by far too tall, the other in Flamboyant Gothic, far too elaborate. But the tomb of Saint Grignion de Montfort in the Romanesque church is plain.

The saint was a Breton, born at the end of the seventeenth century. He was a member of the Society of Jesus. The Jesuits were all-powerful in the France of that time, and their learning had a strong attraction for intelligent children. But their influence was exercised to reinforce the advocates of intolerance, whose triumph was the Revocation of the Edict of Nantes. Protestantism had been strong in Poitou and the West; the flight of the more prosperous, the persecution of the poor peasants who could not escape, had desolated the land. 'They made a desert and called it peace.'—Those who want to learn how that reign of terror affected merciful Christians should read the account of Saint-Simon, who was a devout Catholic, and was horrified. Indeed when the Jesuits had finished, for many religion had ceased to exist. Grignion de Montfort shared to the full the missionary zeal of his order; prevented from going on mission abroad, he directed his enthusiasm to the poor of his own country, for he was a preacher in the old manner of the preaching friars. This got him into trouble with his superiors, and he was able to march through the country summoning the people to pilgrimage, only through the protection of the Bishop of Luçon. He was in his own time a figure of controversy; the policy of the Jesuits was not directed to the salvation of the poor, but to influence over the powerful, and Grignion met with much opposition. He evolved a doctrine of his own based upon what he called the Wisdom of Sainte Marie et de la Croix. Two orders remember him, the Daughters of Wisdom, and the Brothers of Saint Gabriel. The second tall church is the chapel of the Filles de la Sagesse, and near by is the monastery of the Frères de Saint Gabriel, the brother order. The Filles de la Sagesse devote their care to the old and to the very young. They specialize in maternity work and have in past times followed the flag to nurse the wounded in war.

The Porteress of the Abbey, a nun with the dignity and serenity of the religious life in her demeanour, showed me the chapel. The funds to build it were due, she said, to a small property in Paris which was demolished when Haussmann made the boulevards. I admired the intricacy of the Gothic church. 'It will not last,' she sighed. 'It is made of tufa.' She gave me a book recounting the life and work of the saint. He has remained a much-loved figure in the neighbourhood. Both these churches, and the cave in the forest of Vouvant where he lived in solitude for a time, are the bournes of great pilgrimages. The old men of a hospital where he served at Poitiers petitioned to have him sent back to them. 'We humbly beg to make our venerable pastor return, he who so much loves the poor.'

Of the leaders of religion who made the Counter-Reformation in France, Saint Grignion de Montfort was the successor, in a later generation, of Saint Vincent de Paul, who also loved the poor. Their orders still live and work. In Saint Grignion's case some people believe that the steadfast Catholicism of the Vendée still draws from his tradition.

This part of the country holds the tale of another character very different from that of a saint; for he was the most detestable criminal of French history, Gilles de Retz. He was a rich young nobleman of the small court of the Dauphin Charles, one who called cousin with the house of Montmorency, the proudest next to royalty in the realm. With Dunois he was of the party of Jeanne d'Arc, supporting her against the intrigues of the Trimouille faction. With the rising fortune of Charles VII, he had the world as his plaything. But he played too hard. In spite of the ownership of a fistful of castle domains, and of the rich saltings of the coast, he ruined himself, and took to magic to repair his losses. There was nothing odd about this; every king of that time had his personal magician. But Gilles de Retz needed to discover the recipe for the Philosopher's Stone, which would turn base metal into gold. That recipe could be given only by the devil, so he must raise the devil.

His wizards told him that this involved rites in which it was necessary to sacrifice a virgin boy child. Little boys began to disappear from his domains, and the people grew to understand that they were lured to death in the castles of Gilles de Retz. But he was a great noble, with unlimited power over his own lands; the people were too terrified of his actual and his magical power to rise against him. At last a courageous bishop of Nantes accused him. He was tried. The bones of scores of children were found in the underground sewers and dungeons of his castles. He was condemned for sorcery and murder and burned to death.

All this was told me in a sober narrative, by the farmer whose land now contains the castle of Tiffauges. Later he introduced me to his wife and seven children, who received me with great courtesy. One is apt to be told that a castle lived in by Gilles de Retz was one of those built by the fairy Mélusine; and it is true that a collection of castles passed from a cadet line of the Lusignans to the family of de Retz.

France can always be trusted to offer dramatic contrasts in the stories of local notables. This water-logged country of the Retz, which forms the south side of the Loire estuary, is dull in itself. There is however one old abbey at St.-Philbert-de-Grand-Lieu, which holds the tomb transiently occupied by the relics of Saint Philbert. His monks were driven from their abbey of Jumièges on the Seine by Norman raiders; and with what seems like incredible idiocy, they took refuge at Noirmoutier on the island of that name; where inevitably the Normans turned up again. They fled with their precious relics to St.-Philbert-de-Grand-Lieu; but that proved no safer, and finally they went deep inland to the Saone valley and built the marvellous abbey of Tournus. But the memory of the nomadic monks persists; there is a pilgrimage to St.-Philbert-de-Grand-Lieu.

6. SOUTH-WEST FROM POITIERS

A *route nationale* runs from Poitiers south-west to Niort and finally to the sea at La Rochelle. Various interesting places lie on this road or near to it. I shall take it east to west.

Lusignan comes first. The traveller is apt to discount it, because the road runs through a narrow centre street and takes all his attention. The castle has disappeared. It is well to seek the church, which is very fine, with a beautiful Romanesque tower.

Yet Lusignan is full of memories. The Counts of Lusignan were one of the most powerful families of the Middle Ages; the more so that they were of fairy descent. Raimondin, count of the time, met three maidens in a wood. He married the fairest, Mélusine. He had small reason to doubt that she was a fairy, for she built six castles for him, each in a single night. He was worried, all the same, because she would never let him enter her bedchamber on a Saturday. When he burst in, she lay on her bed in her true form, with the horrible long tail of a dragon. She flew out of the window and was never seen again. There were similar tales in the region; for instance the Angevin line included a she-devil of whom they were very proud. I may remark that though I do not remember seeing this in any history-book, many historians must have noticed that the advent of Christianity forced the noble families to revise their descent from gods. Mélusine was a water-goddess, it seems. But whereas till the fall of the Roman Empire all the great clans of Rome declared that they were descended from gods—as Julius Caesar was from Venus—Christianity only allowed for one God-begotten man. So the divine ancestors were demoted to fairies or devils, and did just as well, really.

The most wonderful of late mediaeval Books of Hours, the *Très Riches Heures du Duc de Berry*, portrays the Castle of Lusignan on the hilltop above the fields, with a small but elegant dragon flying above the donjon tower. The Lusignans were allies of the Dukes of Aquitaine, and when Guy de Lusignan married Sybille de Bouillon, one of two princesses who claimed the throne of the Crusader Kingdom of Jerusalem, Richard Coeur-de-Lion supported his friend. In fact Guy soon died; but it was Lusignans who founded the Kingdom of Cyprus, and held it till the Venetian annexation centuries later. Junior branches of the family owned titles and lands hereabouts till the nineteenth century, but the titles of counts of Lusignan and of the Marche passed to the kings of France.

Near by Lusignan to the north-west, lovers of Roman remains will find Sanxay, where the Père de la Croix has excavated the foundations of a theatre and a temple; and lovers of Flamboyant Gothic can see the pretty Aumonerie of Ménigoute.

MELLE

From Lusignan the main road leads by St.-Maixent-l'École to Niort, but a better way to take is by Melle and Celles; rather longer, but much nicer.

Melle is a charming little town with modern industry and no less than three Romanesque churches. It slopes down to the side of the river Béronne, and at its modern summit is a large distillery and a fairground. One of the old churches is disaffected and bare. One, a St.-Pierre, has good carvings both outside and in. But it is the priory of St.-Hilaire that is the best of all. It stands on the west bank of the river with its delightful flock of round-ended chapels showing above the stream surrounded by fruit-trees. It is pleasant to think that it must look today much as it did when it was new. The apple-trees, of course, are not the same; but the monks were the best agriculturalists of their time; no doubt they had orchards too. The abbey is decorated with carvings both outside and in. The fine north door has a Cavalier above it. One walks down from the west door into the nave, which gives that interesting view of the pillars caused by this device. It is the parish church now, and does not have the sad feeling of many deserted abbeys.

CELLES

Celles-sur-Belle was a monastery town. Its church retains a Romanesque door, with grotesque heads caught in the scallops of its 'Saracen' carvings. The interior was restored by Leduc de Toscane, and has the grace of all his work. He adhered to the Gothic style, yet there is a difference. This is his country; he restored the abbey of St.-Maixent-l'École near by; and the region was lucky to have him, for, by comparison with the disastrous Abadie, he was a real architect. It is a solemn thought that Talleyrand was the last commendatory abbot of Celles.

126

7. NIORT AND THE MARAIS POITEVIN

Niort used to be the port of Poitou till the Sèvre-Niortaise sanded up. It was still an important port when the Plantagenets ruled Aquitaine. Henry of Anjou built its great castle. Sir John Chandos lived there as Constable of Aquitaine for Edward III of England. It seems likely that his government, and that of the earlier Edward I when he was Prince of Wales, were the best periods enjoyed by Aquitaine for a long time. My Scottish type-writer almost refuses to write the name of Edward I, the worst enemy Scotland ever had, but justice must be done.

Niort is still a busy market, serving the intensively cultivated country of the dry Marais. Besides its huge double donjon, it has a pretty Renaissance museum, formerly the town hall, and the Church of Notre-Dame, with a tall spire of the end of the Gothic period.

The Sèvre-Niortaise runs to sea to the west of Niort, through the strange region of the Marais de Poitou, the Marsh of Poitou. The Atlantic winds pile up sand at the river-mouth, it struggles to sea with the greatest difficulty and behind its inadequate outlet the water of the wet seasons floods the land. The draining of the marshes began long ago, in the Middle Ages; five abbeys settled round the slightly raised edges of the Marsh and set themselves to redeeming it. Then they ceased their work, and it was not till the reign of Henry IV that he sent to Holland for experts to cut channels to carry off the water. There is still a great drain called *la Ceinture des Hollandais*. The work went on till at the close of the seventeenth century the greater part of the Marsh had been dried; that is, it had been ditched and drained: the whole country looks like a chequer-board of canals. The result is land of great fertility; it is devoted to fine cultivation, such as vegetables, but also grain and beasts, cattle and pigs. It is very dull to look at. The inner Marais is the wet marsh. It is still inundated with the rivers every winter. Not that it is uninhabited; every little rise has a farm upon it, and the innumerable channels and dykes are used to frame fields on which cattle graze in the dry season. The channels are ringed with reeds, and edged with poplars, willows, alders. The people, and the cattle too, travel by flat-bottomed boats.

When I went to the Marais, to Coulon, a boatman took me for an hour's tour of the Marsh. 'Come by this little *veneuil*,' he said, leading me through a passage between houses. 'That's one for the Auld Alliance,' I thought; 'Edinburgh has a Vennel; Perth has two.' Against the bank his boat was moored; it was a punt. 'You will never have seen a boat like this,' said the marshman. I remembered the people whom I taught to punt on the Cherwell at Oxford, and lied in the proper womanly way. 'No, never, 'I said. The marshman told me the history of the drainage of the Marais. 'It used to be fever-stricken. But not now. The dragonflies eat the mosquitoes.' There were indeed masses of dragonflies, of a blue so dark they looked black. And as I had thoughtfully smeared my face and hands with fly-repellent, I listened to a small buzzing sound with calm.

From Niort one can easily reach La Rochelle, but I do not describe it here, because it will come into a later account of the seashore. North of the Marsh is Maillezais, which has a fine ruined abbey in a farm. Agrippa d'Aubigny, the historian of the Wars of Religion, fortified it as a strong-place of the Huguenots. He belonged to this district. At his lonely castle of Mursay on the Sèvre, his daughter brought up the little girl who was much later to be the unacknowledged wife of Louis XIV, and the real queen of France, Françoise d'Aubigny, whom we know as Madame de Maintenon. She harboured a lasting grudge against her aunt, because she made her herd the geese; but I find this grievance beyond my sympathy: what occupation could a girl at Mursay find better than herding geese? Not far away, if you take the Champdeniers road from Niort, is the village of Échiré. Take a lane half-way up that steep village to the left, and you come to Coudray-Salvert, an immense ruined castle, a line of six ivied towers, standing above the Sèvre. Otherwise, in this region, there is the cathedral of Luçon, Richelieu's first bishopric. It is rather an architectural muddle, but has a graceful west façade by Leduc de Toscane.

29. Arch of Germanicus, Saintes

30. Fenioux. West Door

Chapter Nine

THE CHARENTES

1. THE ROAD TO ANGOULÊME

Angoulême lies due south of Poitiers, and an hour's uninteresting drive takes the tourist to the city. He feels he has no time to diverge from that hypnotic stream of traffic. But if he exercises great strength of will, there are unspoiled country and places on either side of the road. About half-way it is crossed by a main road that marks the Seuil de Poitou. The ridge is scarcely noticeable, but the Seuil casts its waters to the south, and they run out to sea as the system of the Charente river. It rises in the small hills of the end of the Limousin plateau, runs north to Civray on the Seuil, turns west and then south to Angoulême; after which it pursues a meandering course westwards to the Atlantic.

Eastwards, the road of the Seuil reaches some old places. One is Civray, which has perhaps the most elaborate of all the Romanesque church façades, a series of superimposed friezes of figures. It is like a theatre curtain, some say; for they think it overloaded. A few miles further east is Charroux, where the ruins of a famous abbey still show three stories of its octagonal tower. It was an abbey built in concentric circles, in imitation of the church of the Sepulchre at Jerusalem, and it still houses some lovely thirteenth-century statues. So they say; for I failed to enter it; I rang the bell for nearly an hour, but no one answered.

Charroux is famous in history because it was there, in 989, that the Council of the Church proclaimed the Pax Dei; the Peace of

God. The councillors sought to confine the bounds of private warfare, a right which the barons still held and constantly used. The clerics forbade the killing of priests, farm labourers, travellers, merchants, women, and plough animals; and the destruction of mills. Later councils worked out the Truce of God, decreeing that war must be suspended on holy days. It seems to me that some historian ought to have studied the evolution of Western Christianity from the total pacifism of the teaching of Jesus in the Sermon on the Mount and on His Cross, to a condition when the Church itself preached and practised war. This is surely the Great Distortion of the faith. No doubt, once Christianity was tolerated by Constantine, and later became the dominant religion, it was faced with a crucial problem of power. No doubt, in the West, it was unfortunate that the Catholic faith was identified with the most bellicose of the conquering barbarians. But the result of history was that the Church and State had combined to turn Christianity inside out and upside down. Even today, you may meet priests who advocate war, if it is waged, as they think, to the advantage of the Church. Nobody would expect the ordinary layman to think much about a moral code he has inherited, and millions of soldiers accept that they are fighting the battles of God. But, after all, the Dark Ages were far nearer in time to the early days when men went to the stake rather than bear arms. There must have been many who sought refuge from the dilemma in the cloister; and many more who were troubled by the conflict between the early faith and its later practice. There is nothing to prove that men were less intelligent in the nine hundreds than they are now; like us they may have listened to arguments in favour of force; and like us they may have found that the more sophisticated those arguments were, the less convincing they became.

The Charente is a slow and drowsy stream; its course is marked in these upper reaches, not by roads, but by the line of trees on its banks. Its farming has been of sheep, through the ages; there are three places close together called Mouton, Moutonneau, and Champagne-Mouton. Sure enough, Mouton has the Lamb of God carved above its church door. In the river-fields near Mansle is Lichères, an abbey lost among the pastures. To my taste it is far more charming than Civray; its delicately pillared apse rises from the cabbages of the surrounding farm.

Further east, beyond a belt of forest, is La Rochefoucauld. The small town is dominated by its castle. The huge donjon tower split a few years ago—from the hill behind it you can see the yawning gap, and till it is made safe, visitors are not admitted. But while the Beaux-Arts are about their work, it remains even from the exterior one of the finest castles in France. The tower is mediaeval, but the courtyard is fine Renaissance; there is a beautifully wrought staircase. Most foreigners connect the name of Rochefoucauld mainly with the writer of the seventeenth century, who fell from favour at court and retired to Verteuil, another castle of his family, to write his cynical Maxims. That was François VI; but in fact there were plenty more notable Rochefoucaulds; a family which has held the same lands for a thousand years is bound to leave traditions. There are still traces of feudalism in the country here. I stopped one day at Verteuil, where Rochefoucaulds still live. At the door of a house in the small terrace beside the park an old woman sat. There was an empty chair at her side; 'Come and sit with me,' she said. I obeyed. 'The castle is not shown', she said. 'I know,' I replied. 'I just wanted to photograph it from the bridge; it is a pretty view.' 'Well, you can have a little chat with me first. I am in form today; sometimes I am not in form for conversation. I am eighty-six.' 'You carry your age well, Madame.' 'Yes! when the day is fine, like this. I have been shown the château. My family has always lived here, but my grandchildren live in Paris. When they came on holiday, I knew that they would love to see the castle. They told me that I should ask a certain person to intervene with the Viscountess for me. But I thought I should approach her directly, so I wrote to her and explained. She invited us all, and she showed us the castle herself. I am sure that I did right.' 'I am sure that you did,' said I. 'It was very kind of her; but of course she knows who I am, for I have always been here.'

The western side of the *route nationale* to Angoulême, which seems to form a frontier difficult to cross, is the valley of the south-ward-curving Charente below Mansle. This country is little visited, and has few things to see. The best centre for it is Aigre, a dull town containing the best hotel I have found in this region, the France, well worth turning aside to seek. There are several villages which have cracked church towers; in one the old abbey of Marcillac is reduced to its apse, and the great chancel-arch lies shattered on the ground. In the apse a plain chair stood beside a table, and on it a jar with a child's bunch of flowers stuffed into it —so they still use the church.

At Javarzay I went into a church which the guidebook describes as 'curious'. As a rule this means old without beauty. The door creaked loudly as I pushed it, and I found that a marriage was being celebrated. In order not to interrupt I sat on a bench concealed from the altar by a pillar. Presently I found my gaze riveted by a plaque on the transept wall. This offered thanks to the Blessed Virgin for her 'Visible Intervention' on June 4th 1944 'without which the people of this place would have suffered the fate of Oradour'. The town of Ménigoute, thirty miles north, has a similar inscription, but outside the church. There is a story here. Who warned the people? The Blessed Virgin, they believe; perhaps we are not yet so far from the spirit of Loudun, where the Virgin met Saint Radegonde in the dark and guided her home.

2. AULNAY

Perhaps the visitor will not have time to explore these remote villages, but there is one place which it is essential to seek, and that is Aulnay. This has the most beautiful church in the whole of Charente—many would say in the whole of South-West France. I should not go so far as that; but it comes very high in any list. And what is especially enjoyable about it is that Aulnay is not a great city, and its church is not a cathedral, but a small town with the perfect town church. The place is not near to anywhere, and you can reach it from Angoulême, or Saintes. It is conveniently attained from Aigre, which is why I place it here.

Aulnay marks the point where the Romanesque architecture of Poitou and Saintonge reached its summit. It is set in a big churchyard outside the town, so that the total grace of the building, crowned by its spire, its slightness repeated by cypress trees, is visible. The actual spire is Gothic, but the rest of the church is Romanesque.

It is best to approach it from the east, in the morning, when the light falls on the slim pillars of the east end. Then the tower, the slender round apse below it with its two attendant chapels, the outstretched arms of the transepts, make an effect of simplicity containing lovely detail which may be the secret of Aulnay. When you draw near to the apse, you see the rarest single beauty of many: the bands of interlaced carving on either side and below the east window. This is of great intricacy and delicacy, the work of a master. The same hand carved the pillar of the east end and the chapels, and I think the south door, but at some point of the sculptures of the exterior another carver began to take over, and the interior carving is clearly the work of another man; it is larger in scale and much simpler in design. All the decorations are of the same style; indeed they must have been the work of a large workshop, but they are not quite of the same date: the south door has a round pure Romanesque arch; the eastern portals are pointed, and so are the arches of the interior roof.

The door of the south transept is famous. It has four rings of carving: the innermost is of monsters interlaced with branches, the next of saints, the third of Elders of the Apocalypse, the outer ring of grotesques, dragons, man-owls, beasts like deer or goats taking church ceremonies—the goblin world of the books called 'Bestiaries'. Above this door a window is flanked by four Virtues leaning on their shields; they are, unusually, figures of men.

The western door has a central portal and, as is common in Poitevin architecture, two blind arches partly filled with carving on either side. The side arches have Christ in Glory, and the crucifixion of Saint Peter, as subjects. The centre door is surrounded by figures slanting up to the pointed arch, the inner line of angels rising to the Lamb of God, the second the Virtues subduing the Vices—in this case, they are female Virtues—the third the Wise and Foolish Virgins, the fourth the labours of the months and the signs of the Zodiac.

One is apt to look at the zodiacal signs and wonder why they play so great a part in the iconography of the Middle Ages; for after all they are magic, and the Church punished the practice of magic with burning at the stake. They must have been considered White Magic—since they made a respectable entry into the Christian story with the visit of the Mages to the manger of Bethlehem. For the Wise Men were not kings, as the snobbery of the Middle Ages imagined them, but Mages, astronomers, followers of a star. From the science of Persia to the computerized babblings of the modern press the line of descent is uninterrupted; the stars foretell the destiny of man.

The interior of Aulnay has the same combination of clear design and masses of sculpture. The pillar capitals are very varied; they include formal patterns, palm-buds, Biblical scenes like the famous Delilah cutting off Samson's hair, animals and monsters. There are several griffin capitals—it is after these capitals that I imagine a carver called 'the Master of the Griffin'. One capital has a procession of elephants walking round it. I believe that his mates wanted to know the nature of those strange beasts. 'Griffins we know; and lions we know; but what are those?' The sculptor carved in large letters below them: 'These are Elephants', '*Hi Sunt Elephantes*'.

First and last, Aulnay owes its excellence to its proportion. This is a grace so rare, and so inexplicable, that it is impossible to analyse. Of course every architect intends to make a beautifully proportioned structure, each time he designs a building. Yet it seems as though sometimes a blest accident happens, and the builder looks at his work and knows that it is better even than his dream.

In the neighbourhood of Aulnay there are a number of old places. Dampierre has a pretty castle; Nouaillé further down the Boutonne a lovely small church, whose doorway is clearly by the workmen of Aulnay, but has not, like Aulnay, been over-restored. Varaize near to St.-Jean-d'Angély is another like it. The traveller must use his eye for those ancient churches; they are usually indicated by their towers; the Michelin maps do not always bother to mark them as interesting.

3. ANGOULÊME

From Mansle to Angoulême the Charente meanders along, often dividing into a multiplicity of branches round islands. If the traveller takes the turn to St.-Amant-de-Boixe he will find a great abbey church, with a pillared west front, and a north transept delicately carved. The interior of the nave is Romanesque, the chancel Gothic.

Angoulême is splendidly situated on a promontory above the Charente. It is crowned by its cathedral, and the crest of the town is entirely surrounded by ramparts. From the river-level, and especially from the west and the south, it has a wonderful skyline. You can walk almost right round the ramparts, from which cliffs fall to the river. They are ascended by three zigzag roads, which must be mastered by trial and error.

The Cathedral is superbly set. It has a tall façade rising up to a gable, and flanked by two towers; and a great belfry tower built on its north transept. The whole front between the towers is elaborately carved. Unfortunately a large part of the carving is not ancient, but a reconstruction by a man called Abadie, a nineteenth-century architect. The towers and the gable of the west front are his; the upper carvings and the top of the portal. It is necessary to say something about Abadie. He was roughly contemporary with Viollet-le-Duc, and was, like him, employed to repair many great buildings. But while Viollet-le-Duc was a scholarly and conscientious antiquarian, so that his work is at least faithful to its periods, Abadie was not. His abounding imagination prompted him to tear down anything that did not attract him and to substitute his own fancies. To have done this on the scale of his alterations to Angoulême Cathedral denotes a staggering self-confidence, totally unjustified. His heavy hand was laid on many treasures hereabouts; he did not spare Aulnay; he rebuilt the lovely little octagonal church of St.-Michel near Angoulême so that the most ignorant beholder can see how spoilt it is. I apologize, but the pun is irresistible; Abadie was a Baddy.

The authentic carvings of Angoulême are the Last Judgment on the western front. Angels and saints rise to the Tree of Life below the Christ in Judgment. The sculpture is of the style known as the school of Toulouse, which is found in the churches of Périgord. The angels dance in an aerial ballet, their wings bending them backward at the waist. The interior of the church is Périgourdin also, for the roof is a series of domes.

Round the corner from the Cathedral is a delightful old house, that used to be the bishop's palace; it is a museum. It contains a remarkable collection of African sculpture; the best I remember seeing anywhere. There is not a great deal of old work otherwise in Angoulême, save one Romanesque tower, and two towers of the Town Hall, which Abadie kindly left when he pulled down the old castle of the Counts. One of the towers is named for Marguerite, the presiding spirit of Angoulême.

There was an earlier lady, Isabelle d'Angoulême, who also became a queen. She was heiress of the county, and a great matrimonial prize. She was betrothed to the Lusignan Count de La Marche. But John Lackland of Anjou practically abducted her—there can be no question of a love-affair, she was only a child—and married her. When he succeeded in capturing his nephew Arthur of Brittany, tearing the boy from the protection of his grandmother Eleanor of Aquitaine and murdering him, he became king of England. In 1316 John died, and the Poitevin lady became guardian of her son Henry III in a land ruled by Normans who had no liking for Poitevins. In the end she returned to her native country, and married her original fiancé, the Count de La Marche. She had to watch the domains of the Lusignans, and the castles of Mélusine, successively taken and annexed by the French king Philippe Auguste. She cried out that her people were being reduced to slavery, but in vain. Philippe II, the idol of the centralist French historians, was a rapacious conqueror, but an able general. In the end, Isabelle was remembered as the Queen of England; and she was carried to the Abbey of Fontrevault to lie with the Plantagenet kings.

Angoulême is far more aware of its other leading lady, Marguerite d'Angoulême. She was the sister of François I, who succeeded to the throne as the male heir of his cousin Louis XII. Marguerite is the type of the devoted sister; all her life she lived for François, regarding her queenship of Navarre as a minor consideration. But she was worth at least twice as much as the disastrous François. Even in his one good trait, his love of art, she surpassed him; he collected Italian artists, she wrote: hymns with one side of her nature—for she inclined to the Reform—the scurrilous tales of the *Heptaméron* with the other, the side of the Renaissance intellectual. Had she but been born the senior and a man, France would have had its Renaissance without the inglorious tale of the Italian wars, and with a tolerance which might have avoided the civil Wars of Religion. Marguerite bequeathed her wit and her tolerance to her grandson Henri IV of France and of Navarre. Unluckily they were not transmitted to her further kindred, saving her great-great-grandson, Charles II of England.

4. NEAR ANGOULÊME

I was sitting in the lounge of the Hôtel du Palais at Angoulême when a man spoke to me. He looked the sort of Englishman who retires to the country after a life of work in London. He had been on pilgrimage to Lourdes, he told me. 'Is it not extraordinary to find a pure Roman church here in the heart of France?' he said. I murmured something about there being many Romanesque churches in the neighbourhood; and then we parted.

Indeed the Romanesque churches of the Charentes are numbered not by the dozen but by the score. I do not propose to give tedious lists of them—and in any case I have not seen a tithe of them—for they are a life-time's study. But I shall please my fancy by picking out a few. The traveller must just use his curiosity in exploration, and may feel justly that he has found far better ones than I have.

First it is better to take minor roads, for the best villages are not upon the main ones. For this reason many people who have travelled in the Charente say 'We saw only a few of those old buildings; they are no more common than anywhere else in France.' But this is a mistake; one has to turn off to places which are hardly villages, and at the end of a lane one is confronted by a lonely abbey.

Not that the roads are to be despised, in themselves. One of the roads south from Angoulême runs eventually to Périgueux. It is a lovely route to take south to Brantôme on the river Dronne. Brantôme is a delicious little town with an excellent hotel. From there you can follow the river downstream to Bourdeilles with its high castle, to Aubeterre which has a strange church carved out of the rock underground— a monolithic church, the French call it. Then you must keep to the right bank of the Dronne all the way to Coutras, the town where Henri of Navarre won his first victory against the Ligue, the extreme Catholic army. The Huguenots had two cannon, and when you see the steep hills up which they had to manhandle them, you wonder how they did it; but of course they had the white plume of Navarre, too. You may like to spend the night at Libourne, going this way to Bordeaux. It is a nice bastide, now a wine-town, with a good inn; and others besides me may think driving in Bordeaux is enough to send one crazy.

This lovely river, the Dronne, is not the only way south. A road runs from Angoulême to Chalais along a ridge with parallel valleys where there are small ancient churches on either hand. For instance, Plassac, near Blanzac, is my ideal of a village church; Romanesque in miniature, as perfect in its way as Aulnay. Yet Plassac is hardly a village; it is a scattering of tiny houses; six or seven of them. It qualifies for the term *'agglomération'* which France uses to describe a collection of three houses or more; and which is used with enormous relish by French road-police. For nobody enjoys making fun of pompous French official language more than French officials. Well, Plassac can never have been more than a hamlet; yet its church has an elegant pillared façade, a tower turning from a circle to an octagon, and finely carved pillar capitals inside.

Châteauneuf down-river from Angoulême has a lovely tall church and is a good centre for exploration to the south; the country is called first 'Champagne' and later, as it nears Coutras, 'Le Double'. It has great space, among the woody valleys, great peace, because it holds small places and just enough farming population to sustain the little market-towns. I remember driving

once on a road through fields and woods where there was no
other car for miles, and saying to myself, 'It is because it is so quiet
that I feel so happy.' Then I realized the reason for that joy: there
were no wires along the road, and not a post; overhead there were
only the spring clouds blowing across a clear sky. This is deep,
deep country.

5. COGNAC AND CHÂTRES

If you cross the river at Châteauneuf, you come immediately
into the domain of Cognac. The whole country of the north of the
river is devoted to the production of brandy-wine so that the
name of Cognac has become almost identified with brandy. One
meticulously cultivated vineyard gives place to another, but the
influence of the culture reaches for many miles beyond the city.
First the vineyards, in order of precedence, according to the nature
of the soil, from the vineyards of *grande champagne* and *petite
champagne* to the *bois communs*. It is a wide territory, reaching from
the Sèvre-Niortaise to the Dordogne, for the purposes of the
industry; for the brandy hierarchy have made rules, such as that for
the oak of which barrels may be made; it must come from this area
and none other. However it is near to Cognac that the *chais*, the
winestores, begin to appear. They are pleasing buildings, two or
three stories high and massive, so that they give an even tempera-
ture to the stores. Each is surrounded by a high wall, with one tall
arched gate, to allow the piled vans to pass, and the great wooden
doors to be locked after them. I pay a great deal of attention to
new buildings in France, hoping to see some new architecture that
is worth admiration. It is a great pleasure to say that one sort of
structure is very fine indeed, and that is the modern *chais*. It is
traditional in line, but so functional and suited to the soil that it
seems to have grown there. There are some new *chais* in the Cognac
neighbourhood, built, so I was told, to house the distilleries of the
pineau, an after-dinner drink made by blending brandy and wine.

Cognac itself is rather an ugly town, by the high standards of
these parts. Its streets are packed with traffic where every driver
looks anxious and in a hurry to get away. The brandy distilleries

make a roll of great names, like Martel, Hennessy, Prince de Polignac, Courvoisier, Grand Marnier. Some of the *chais* are open to visitors. I chose Martel, because of its situation at the top of the river-bank town, and saw the distillery in company with about sixty other people. We were guided by a Personage resembling an archbishop, who told us in clear and measured tones what it behoved us to learn, no more, no less. The wine is first set in great tanks to ferment, then it is distilled and redistilled, then kept in barrels for at least five years to mature; it is the oaken staves of the barrels that give it its pale golden tint. Then it is bottled. The nice part of the visit, for me, was the long gallery where old wise-looking coopers were tending the barrels, seeing that they were clean and perfect, and paying no more attention to us than if we were flies on the wall. Also the guide took us to the roof and let us look over the long stretch to the north of this kingdom of wine. But the great labelling hall was terrible to me. It was deafening with the din of machinery; the bottles lay on moving bands which paused at every so many seconds to allow a woman to stick on a label. The women were dressed in overalls of a beautiful Chinese blue. Back at the stately reception-room we were each given a small flask of Martel brandy. That was gratifying, and it was all very instructive; and it ill became me to find the exposition of brandy-manufacture exhausting, for it is the only liqueur that I enjoy.

The making and export of brandy is relatively modern, dating from about the seventeenth century. Its present export is of course enormous. But long before it was thought of, except as the private barrel of eau-de-vie which every farmer made for the use of his own family, the valley of the Charente was closely populated. If you take the road from Châteauneuf to Cognac and beyond, keeping as close to the river as the roads allow, you find old places that look as they must have done for centuries. One is Bassac where the abbey has a curious Oriental-seeming door of the sort called 'trilobed'—'*porte trilobée*'—or Bourg-Charente, a very pretty village with a perfect Périgourdin domed church.

From the village of St.-Brice, near Cognac, a small road runs over a woody hill. At the top are the remains of a castle with a romantic name, Garde-Epée, now occupied as farm-buildings. It was a Thursday, and several small children released from school were playing in the courtyard of the castle. I stopped, whereupon they vanished like rabbits into the granges, but I managed to arrest a little boy and ask him the way to the church. He waved his fat arm vaguely downhill, and on the slope I found a farm gate opening on a footpath. It ran down through the wood to a stream crossed by stepping-stones. Beyond them stood the abbey, the water-meadow framing its enchanted solitude. It was Notre-Dame-de-Châtres, once; now it is a barn.

It is tall, bare, pure. Its height is denoted by cypress-trees growing beside it. It has a façade of ranges of pillars, and a white trilobed door. A notice is set on a stake inside the door saying 'no admittance'. I stood and gazed at this magical church, my mind weaving a story to explain why an abbey should have been built by the stream so near to the castle on the hill; was the seigneur a friend of the abbot, perhaps? Had they grown up together as pages at the court of the lord of Cognac? I became conscious of the sound of running footsteps in the woods, and of a series of Red Indian whoops, and turned to see a band of children at the stepping-stones. Like a perfect fool I did not ask them to tell me the story of the abbey, and of the castle from which they had collected their forces to defend their church from invasion. I only said—for there were eleven of them, all under twelve years old—'You cannot be all of one family?' 'No,' said a bright boy who acted as their leader. 'We are three families.' We talked about this, sorting out the families, two fours and a threesome. By good luck, I had a bag of sweets in my car, and I gave it to the leaders for distribution, hoping that they would not think me mean. Their protection of their abbey was executed with the precision of long practice, I admired it very much. And all visitors to lonely abbeys are not as law-abiding as British spinsters.

Chapter Ten

SAINTONGE

———————◦>◦◊◦<◦———————

1. SAINTES

The departments of the Charentes, in our times, consist of Charente and Charente-Maritime. But the old names usually have more meaning. This is certainly true of Saintonge, which means the land of the Santones, the Celts who were here when the Romans came. Its capital is Saintes. I find it difficult to write judicially about Saintes, for to me it is a beloved city.

The Charente here is a big, strong river; running south to north in its complicated course to the sea. Coming from Cognac, you suddenly see the river in its valley, and the spires and towers of the town. The slope downhill becomes a wide street, tree-lined, and you reach the bridge; over it the avenue runs straight uphill, east to west, between modern shops; after half a mile you are at the end of the city. For all that central avenue shows, except for the river, Saintes might be quite commonplace.

But it is easy to be mistaken about old cities. Just on the Cours National beyond the bridge a turn leads to the Hôtel Commerce. This hotel typifies for me the virtues of Saintes. Its hosts, Monsieur and Madame Baty, give the guest a charming welcome, as though they were truly pleased to see her. This cannot of course be more than a convention of good hotel-keeping; but it is a graceful convention. The hotel is comfortable, dead quiet at night; it has a good restaurant. But above all, for me, it has a Romanesque lion sitting on a pedestal in its hall. He is small but authentic; he must have supported a saint, I think, for his face bears an expression of idiotic adoration.

To the south of the Cours National, full of cafés, radio-shops, tourist souvenirs, lies old Saintes. It is a maze of narrow streets, with many old houses, every here and there a Renaissance or mediaeval window or door, till the streets end at the Musée Mestreau, a good museum of local archaeology on the Place Bel-Air. Within this old town there are three of the sights of Saintes. The first is the Arènes, a very large Roman amphitheatre, carved out of a natural oval-ended ravine. It is here that Saintes celebrates a festival of drama every August. Above the ravine stands the church of St.-Eutrope. This was a great Romanesque church, but it has lost its nave. It has a magnificent Gothic spire, given to it by Louis XI. But under the church is the crypt that is the glory of St.-Eutrope. He was in life the third-century evangelist of Saintes, and his tomb is in the crypt. It is illuminated by means of putting a new franc in a slot, when you can see the squat pillars of the crypt, with capitals carved with an extraordinary profusion of plants.

Downhill nearer to the river is the former cathedral, St.-Pierre. It is one of those churches which has been built at various dates—for instance it has a fine Gothic portal, and Flamboyant tower. The whole effect of the cathedral is heavy. The most beautiful church of Saintes, on the east side of the river, is the church of Ste.-Marie-des-Dames. This was a nunnery in Romanesque times, served as a cavalry-barracks till the twentieth century and has now been restored to the church. The Abbey des Dames is a most beautiful church. It is Romanesque, the arcaded west front adorned with delicate carvings. It has a tower of storied pillars. Inside it has a wide nave without aisles, so that it gives a feeling of serene space; the choir is semicircular, lit by windows connected by arcaded pillars. Detail like this has no power to convey the grace and peace of the lovely place.

Beside the bridge there is a big Roman Arch dedicated to Tiberius, as Saintes is reluctant to admit, preferring to call it after Germanicus. Indeed the people of Saintes are rather coy about their prosperous period under the Romans; they do not like to tell you that the Gaulish prince who erected the arch also built an amphitheatre for Lyons. With the tendency to transfer modern nationalism to the past that many teachers import into history, they regard this prince as a Quisling.

2. FÊTE DES ARÈNES GALLO-ROMAINES

Each year, Saintes celebrates a drama festival in the Arènes. In 1965 I went there especially to see it. To my disappointment, it turned out to be the *Bourgeois Gentilhomme* of Molière. I had cherished hopes of *Phèdre*. Like most British girls I had been subjected to the *Bourgeois Gentilhomme* at school, because it is considered suitable for the well-brought-up young. Anyhow I am not fond of Molière; I find the quinine bitterness of his humour distasteful. Moreover, on the day of the presentation it was raining.

'Don't worry!' said Monsieur Baty; 'it'll clear up. It always does for the fête. It'll be dark up there. My son will conduct you.'

Sure enough, it did stop raining. A three-quarters moon was wandering through clouds as the younger Baty took me up the dark streets to the arena. We stumbled down the stepped seats in pitch darkness. The Romans, who seem to have been small men, always made their steps ridiculously high. Arrived on the floor of the theatre, I was conducted to my seat by a young girl. The seats were all on the flat; the immense space was packed with people.

The stage was set at the narrow end of the oval, before the arched entrances to the seats. It was a plain platform with a Louis XIV pavilion at each side. A radiogram played music of Lulli, rather faintly.

The play opened with the discourses of the tutors on deportment. Then the Bourgeois Gentilhomme appeared and advanced at a leisurely pace to the front. He looked at us and smiled. We laughed and clapped and laughed. Louis Seigner, they told me, had made the Bourgeois his own. My slight dislike of the play melted like butter in the sun. Monsieur Seigner was the Bourgeois. That vast confiding smile revealed the whole man; vainglorious, ambitious, snobbish, shrewd in his own affairs, innocent and gullible in the world of fashion of which he was entirely ignorant.

31. Abbey of Notre-Dame-de-Châtres, Grand-Epée

32. La Rochelle. The Old Port

33. Summer Shadows. Magnac-Laval

34. Moûtier-d'Ahun. Bridge of the Creuse

He did not need to say a word. But of course the words followed—
when the audience would let him speak them. The acting was as
perfectly professional as one expects from the Comédie Française.
The audience knew the play by heart, and applauded each well-
known scene. Every wife on the floor approved the tart common-
sense of Madame Jourdain, everybody recognized a friend in the
servant Nicole. It became clear that the play was not only about
poor silly Monsieur Jourdain, whom indeed we all grew to love
for his very innocence, but about the extraordinary society of the
Grand Siècle, where an unclimbable barrier was set between the
well-bred and the bourgeois (unless the bourgeois bought himself
an aristocratic son-in-law by dowering his daughter with a great
fortune, when she might be admitted into a good family, on
sufferance; but her father, never.) But Molière is much harder on
the people who fleece Monsieur Jourdain, the tutors, the false
adventurer gentleman, the false vicomtesse. After all the whole
thing is a masque. In the last act Monsieur Jourdain is deceived
by the offer of a Turkish rank of '*Mamamouchi*'. Under the pale
moon, Turkish hordes began to pour out of the entrances behind
and above the stage; very small Turks first, then larger and larger
children by the hundred. They all wore baggy white trousers,
and immense white turbans; they marched with a prancing
Turkish step. They advanced on Monsieur Jourdain like the
waves of a spring-tide, they overwhelmed him and bore him to the
ground.

No wonder the arena held thousands of spectators! All the
children of Saintes were submerging the Bourgeois. All the mothers
and fathers and aunts and cousins of the population were cheering
in the auditorium. We wiped our eyes and picked our way out of
the Arènes, and home.

3. NEAR TO SAINTES

Saintes is not far from the sea, for the long estuary of the Gironde runs in to the south-east scarcely twenty-five miles away.
But the surrounding country is not maritime, but rural. The
marshes and beaches are beyond a belt of river and woodland.

There are numbers of interesting places within easy reach of
Saintes. The main road to Rochefort by the left side of the Charente
is dull, but near to it is the delightful château de la Rochecourbon,
open to visitors. It is part mediaeval, part seventeenth century. Its
formal gardens include amiable neo-classical statues, of lulloping
figures that would seem to be the goddesses of the Judgment of
Paris, if you could distinguish their attributes through a veil of
thick green moss. Lakes and balustraded 'water-pieces' reflect the
towers. Inside the castle there is a lot of good antique furniture.

The country south of Saintes has a surprising number of villages
—surprising because it is difficult to see what they live upon.
Many of them have old churches. Rioux is the most famous, for it
has a majestic Romanesque apse. For myself I prefer Chadenac.
The untouched Renaissance church of Lonzac was built by Galiot
de Gonouillac, the armourer of Francis I. He decorated it with his
punning motto *'J'aime Fort Une'*, to celebrate both his wealth and
his wife. All those villages are round about Pons, a little town built
upon a conical hill. It is topped by a tall tower, all that remains of
the famous castle that foiled even Richard Coeur-de-Lion, and
whose master was arrogantly called just *'Le Sieur de Pons.'*

If the traveller has only one day to spend in excursions from
Saintes he should take the road north by the right side of the
Charente. At Taillebourg he should diverge by Annepont, and
find Fenioux. This is perhaps the prettiest Romanesque church in
the whole region of this book. It cannot be called a village church,
for there is no village, save a couple of houses. It stands in a small
forest glade. It has a wonderful spire, and a porch flanked by
clustered pillars, surmounted by a row of seven saints, and carved
in its arch with the Virtues and Vices and the Wise and Foolish
Virgins. There is, too, a very grand Lanterne des Morts in the
churchyard.

Fenioux has a line of rosettes binding its carving in the portal.
This gives me an excuse to tell my own tiny contribution to the
story of architectural origins. I have long believed that the formal
designs of art are based upon natural objects. Yugoslav weavers
taught me long ago to interpret the abstract-seeming patterns of
rugs, so that one can say 'This is a spider; this a crab.' Now one of

the most common designs in Romanesque art is the rosette. This is not a rose, but a sort of marguerite. But it is not the clear white marguerite of western Europe, whose petals narrow to points at their ends. The petals of the rosette are wider at the circumference than at the centre, so that the flower fits neatly into a square without leaving a margin of space such as Romanesque carving abhors. I first became familiar with this pattern in eighteenth-century Edinburgh, on the ceilings of plaster-work copied from the work of Robert Adam. For he had collected designs in Italy from the Roman excavations of Pompeii, which the Italians called 'grotesques'. That takes the rosette back to the Roman Empire. Then I happened on a French book about Syria, which had a photograph of a very ancient goddess wearing a diadem shaped like a Russian court lady's coif; it was entirely formed of rosettes. Lastly, in an archaeological work on the Middle East, there was a picture of a great ramp leading up to a palace at Persepolis, and its ascent was carved with a line of enormous rosettes. This seems to me to prove that at least one of the Christian decorations was Eastern and far older than Christianity. But what was my delight, when I was in the island of Rhodes one May, to walk through meadows in the uplands covered with the original rosette, a marguerite with broad-ended petals, their creamy white dusty with golden pollen. Here was indeed the natural flower from which the design is copied.

Chapter Eleven

THE SEASHORE

—————————⟫•❦•⟪—————————

1. PORNIC, SABLES D'OLONNE, LA ROCHELLE

The astute reader may have wondered why this book has followed many roads that lead to the Atlantic shore, without ever reaching it. I have pondered this long, and come to the conclusion that it is simpler to follow the coast from the Loire estuary to the Gironde, instead of coming to each *plage* separately from the inland country. It seems to me that tourists who want to see the inland places may be of somewhat different tastes from those who want to bask on beaches. On the other hand I sometimes imagine parties of father and mother and two or three children. In such cases the parents may like to park the children in a place where they can bathe or sail, and wander about the interior by themselves.

The coast has two main aspects. First there is the shore as a means of earning a livelihood, by deep-sea fishing or by the culture of the shallows. Then there is the pleasure-sea, the long miles of sand, and the sailing or motor-boats for visitors.

The tourist may be surprised by the extent of the maritime industry. Many bays are devoted to the cultivation of oysters and shell-fish like mussels. Oysters, for instance, need shallow water which the tide does not leave dry; and yet which is purified by inflowing springs of fresh water. The longshore farmers have built tanks, sometimes for long stretches of the shore, in which these conditions can be fulfilled. The oyster fisheries are therefore unsuitable for holidays, for they take up the beaches. Marennes and the shallow inlet that runs from it may produce the best oysters of France, but there is little attraction in a shore where even the walls are built of oyster-shells.

The fisheries result in great supplies of excellent fish to eat. If I am in doubt what to order from a menu, I nearly always find myself asking for sole. This is surprisingly cheap, when you think what it costs in restaurants of the interior; but there is a great flat-fish catch in the shallow edges of the sandy Atlantic. In the same way all the shell-fish abound; not only oysters but lobsters, prawns and the best of all, the little shrimps.

There are islands at intervals down this coast, but it must be said that they are not very interesting as islands go. Only one of them, the Ile d'Yeu, is a rocky island; it is the last outpost of the Vendée hills. The rest are sandy, or soil, and are rather closely inhabited and cultivated. The most northerly, the Ile de Noirmoutier, is connected with the mainland by a causeway above water for three hours each low tide.

One or two of the small ports, like Croix de Vie, are picturesque but, as they are occupied in canning fish, they are not really desirable as holiday haunts. Others are partly fishery ports and partly *plages;* these are the most attractive of the seaside towns; and there are a few which are entirely summer-holiday places.

The hotels, varying from *de luxe* caravanserais to relatively simple inns, are pretty dear; for they have to make their living for the year out of a season barely three months long; but as this is a constant factor in seaside places, it will astonish nobody. The French, however, hate the inflated prices of hotels, and they tend to rent or buy a *châlet* where the car can be garaged under the house. Of course this is cheaper than paying hotel bills for a family. The *châlets,* at any rate those that have been built since the last war, are often very pretty. They have adopted the Basque style of house, with the garage and play-room on the ground floor, and bedrooms above. One room always is open to the view, and makes a sun-room. Of course there is a great organization of camps and caravan-sites.

Now I propose to say a few prejudiced words about some of the seaside places. The furthest north where I have stayed is Pornic, on the coast of the Pays de Retz. It is delightfully pretty, built on either side of a river-mouth. It is a fishing-port, and the sands are small.

Les Sables d'Olonne are both commercial and tourist. The port has a long history, some of it bloodthirsty, as when the bourgeois side of the port was Catholic and the fisher side Protestant in the Wars of Religion. Like other ports, Sables d'Olonne were garrisoned by the Germans in the last war, and, as also happened elsewhere, the garrisons were cut off by the advance of the American forces along the Loire Valley. In some towns, the garrisons waited till they were able to surrender and go away peaceably. Here, however, they tried to hold out, and when they were finally driven out they blew up as much of the harbour as they could. There is a nice old harbour, where the fishing-boats and cargo-ships come in to moor, for Sables are the port of the Vendée. The tourist promenade runs for a mile and a half to the south, and is a popular and not very fashionable *plage*.

South of les Sables d'Olonne the coastal region is occupied by the dry part of the Marais Poitevin. This is redeemed land, drained from the marshes and shore; intensively farmed, and quite without scenic interest. It surrounds the bay called L'Anse d'Aiguillon, and there is really no place of interest till you reach La Rochelle.

Here indeed there is interest, especially for English travellers, for La Rochelle in closely interwoven with English history. It is an old city, the capital of the region called 'Aunis' by the people. For the centuries of the Capet and Valois wars with the Plantagenets, it was the prize of victory. The seamen and merchants, who were the Rochelais, were fiercely independent of any outside rulers. They staged one rebellion against the hated salt-tax, the Gabelle, in the sixteenth century, and were massacred by the Constable Anne de Montmorency. They were, for the most part, Protestants in the Wars of Religion, and stood a siege by the royal army because they sheltered refugees from the country-wide slayings that followed the Massacre of Saint Bartholomew. This left deep scars, and when England declared war on France in the reign of James I the Rochelais declared themselves the ally of England. Louis XIII and Richelieu marched to subdue the town in 1627. The Duke of Buckingham commanded the fleet that sailed to support the besieged Protestants, but only got the length of occupying the Ile de Ré at the harbour mouth; for the French forces built a bar across the port's entry and all round the town's land side; it was one of the first works of Vauban. The besieged, under their mayor, Guiton, who is still the saint and hero of La Rochelle, held out till the town starved; when he surrendered there were only nineteen men left who could stand upright. Louis had the sense to make terms with them; but La Rochelle has never forgotten.

As to the British fleet, it had to hoist sails and return to Southampton.

La Rochelle recovered from the siege, because of its superb situation and the skill of its sailors. They were largely responsible for the early colonization of the West Indies, Louisiana, and Canada. Many of the French-Canadians were Calvinists, as was Champlain, the founder of Quebec, who came from Brouage, near by. Later, France forbade Protestants to settle in the colonies.

La Rochelle has kept its reputation for bravery intact. In the last war it was a centre of resistance, despite heavy German occupation. The Germans shot the mayor, who was seventy-six years old.

It is a glorious town, one of the most beautiful of France. And it is far from a museum of antiquities, for it is an important fishing and trading port. The old harbour is too shallow for modern ships; they moor at La Pallice, the modern port round the point. So La Rochelle has been spared the hideous buildings of modern commerce—and in the war the Allies concentrated their bombing on La Pallice, where the Germans had a large submarine-base.

The old harbour has three great towers guarding its mouth, dating from the Middle Ages. Two of them, the Tour de la Chaine and the Tour St.-Nicolas, could stretch a chain across the harbour mouth; the third and tallest, the Tour de la Lanterne, served as a lighthouse. The Grosse Horloge, the Great Clock, is in one of the old town gates on the quay. The chief building is the Hôtel de Ville. It is of the date of Henry IV, and very decorative, if somewhat too well reconstructed. It typifies La Rochelle that its people cherish that council meeting-place, for it means all their history to them. There is a cathedral, but it is a heavy seventeenth-century building, with an air of being alien and unwelcome to the town—but this may only be reading into the architecture of the time the fact that it was set up as a symbol of Louis XIII's victory.

There are many old houses and old streets. The houses are mostly modest in size, though there are streets where the great merchant families live, as they have for centuries, hidden behind forecourts, with walled gardens behind them; these are large enough. Several of the streets are arcaded—the arcades are called '*Porches*' here—so that the people can walk in shelter even if it is raining. It is often raining in La Rochelle. It is a town where you can wander pleasurably for hours. But it is at its lively best when the cafés on the quay, the Cours Wilson, are full at the hour of the aperitif, in the evening, especially if the tide is flowing. For the pool fills with yachts and fishing-boats as close as it can pack, making a scene of such gaiety and beauty that it is impossible to stop watching it.

Yachting is a passion with young France. It is no longer a sport for the rich, followed only round a few fashionable places on the Channel or the Riviera. It is practised by thousands of people sailing yachts or steering motor-boats. The sandy islands of the Atlantic coast are very useful to them, for they can run for shelter if the sea gets up too much; and of course the Atlantic can be stormy. I find it entertaining to watch the effect of a new amusement like this in France; the young people are mad about it, as they are in fact about sport in general. Nobody is more fanatical about mountaineering than a French climber; and nobody more addicted to the sea than a boy who shares a small yacht with his friends.

2. SURGÈRES AND BROUAGE

Surgères is on the road from La Rochelle to Angoulême. It is always a very busy town, for it is the centre of the trade in milk of the Aunis. It founded the cooperation of farmers of the region, and was the pioneer of the processing of dried milk and dairy products. It is like a village that has grown greatly in size without losing its peasant character. Having driven twice through its one-ways in search of a restaurant. I was baffled, when I saw two people entering a house. I asked the way to the church, opposite to which the Michelin map marked a hotel. The man said, 'Well, you have happened on the right passer-by; I used to be the secretary of the Syndicat d'Initiative. I will direct you to the Trois Piliers, and if you come to fetch me after lunch I will show you the church.' I obeyed his directions, and returned to collect him after lunch. He took me to the tree-grown park in which the old church stands. 'Mademoiselle, I am ashamed to show it to you,' he said. 'They have spoiled it with restoration.' The Romanesque church has a fine façade, with arcaded carvings, the central door has decorated arches on either side, and the upper story two Cavaliers.

'They are restored,' moaned my kind guide. 'We found the mouldings in a barn of the castle. I have stored them in the museum.' He showed me the plaster moulds in the small part of the castle which remains. It is visible at once that if the original carvings are covered with plaster in moulds, and the casts thus obtained used to replace the old sculptures, they lose the sharpness and delicacy of the originals; the sea-serpent of Surgères is more like a slug. 'Restored! Restored!' My friend bade me goodbye.

I walked round the big church. It has a fine tower made of sixteen very tall pillars, bound at the top by arches. But the cornice has split, and a pinetree has rooted in the crack, which it will force wider apart with every rainy season. Presently the tower will fall. This fault is common to many churches in Poitou, where the coping has been neglected.

I am ambivalent about restoration. I think it wicked to allow the spires of churches to crumble. But I also think that it is wicked to let restorers as coarse-minded as Abadie loose on Romanesque sculpture. One can but hope that the restorers of today will have too much judgement to produce work such as this which broke the heart of the citizen of Surgères.

South from La Rochelle a road runs by the coast to Rochefort, a town built like a bastide in a chequer-board of streets. It used to be an important naval port, and it is still a centre of training for naval air-pilots. It is a sad place, it seems to me. One can cross the Charente, which runs out to sea here in rather a soiled and unworthy way, by the Pont Transbordeur de Martrou. This is quite an experience. The bridge is a platform on which twelve cars can fit themselves; the platform is swung on cables attached to overhead rails; and the raft swims across the river by those rails. The land beyond this is marshland drained from the sea, with ditches round each field, cattle grazing the salt turf, and across the saltings, the fortress of Brouage.

This is indeed a bastide, only far later in date than the bastides of Périgord. Its fortifications are seventeenth century. Richelieu had them rebuilt. He was governor of the place and wanted to use it, if need be, against the dangerous people of La Rochelle. Brouage had been a rival in trade of La Rochelle, but Condé blocked up its port during the Wars of Religion, and the harbour silted up. It is now about two miles from the sea. It retains exactly the shape of Richelieu's time, a square of walls and three fortified gates. Outside the bastions of the walls are small round turrets, from which enemies approaching could be enfiladed. It is extremely pretty, like a child's dream of a fortress. But this place, whose garrison used to be six thousand soldiers, now has a bare hundred of inhabitants; and many of the houses are in ruins.

Brouage was the scene of a love-tragedy of the young Louis XIV. When he grew up his first affair was with one of the nieces of the all-powerful Cardinal Mazarin, Richelieu's successor and the minister of the Queen, Anne of Austria. Mazarin, an Italian bourgeois, had amassed an enormous fortune out of the pickings of power, and was prepared to buy princely husbands for his five nieces. But when Louis fell deeply and honourably in love with a second niece, Marie de Mancini, the most intelligent of them, and they actually wanted to marry, Mazarin faced a crisis. The nobles of France were quite rebellious enough against the centralized rule organized by Richelieu, and the accompanying decay of their power. They had already shown their dissatisfaction in the Wars of the Fronde. If Mazarin had allowed the king to marry his middle-class niece, there would have been no holding them; and besides he and the Queen were negotiating for Louis to marry a Spanish Infanta, his cousin. Mazarin sent Marie and one of her sisters to Brouage and imprisonment. Louis, dragged round France on a propaganda progress to end with his marriage on the Bidassoa, was inconsolable. He wrote, he sent Marie a puppy, the offspring of his favourite bitch. Marie, well aware that her uncle meant business, did not reply to the letter, and would not adopt the puppy. She read; she pined; she spent hours on the battlements of Brouage, looking at the burning sunlight on the sea. Mazarin learned that the royal party on their return would pass rather near to Brouage; and anyhow Louis was safely though reluctantly married. He took his nieces back to Paris. As the court travelled back, and stopped at St.-Jean-d'Angely, Louis escaped and rode to Brouage, but the Mancini girls were gone. He slept in Marie's room, and gazed on the sea as she had done, and returned to his unloved wife. Mazarin afterwards disposed of Marie to an Italian prince, a Colonna, and Louis waited till Mazarin died, and never had a chief minister again.

3. ROYAN AND BLAYE

Next, to the south, lies Royan at the western point of the Gironde, with the Ile d'Oléron as its continuation. Between Oléron and the mainland there is the Strait of Maumusson, then the Pointe de la Coubre. Then the coast turns south-east and runs in a long stretch of dunes called La Côte Sauvage, with a strip of forest land backing them, to Royan. This is just opposite to the Pointe de Grave, the promontory of the other side of the Gironde, three miles away.

Royan is the fashionable *plage* of all Aquitaine north of the Garonne. It is almost entirely new. It was practically wiped out in the War, and by a dreadful irony it was destroyed not by the Germans, but by the planes of France's allies and by the army of France. The Germans, as elsewhere, had garrisoned Royan and built the 'Atlantic Wall' of strong-points all along the coast. After the retreat of the main German army, pockets of forces were left in the sea-ports. In most cases these were induced to negotiate and depart, when they realized that their position was hopeless. But in Royan they stuck to their posts. The Canadian-trained Royal Air Force was ordered to intimidate them by bombing the light-house of the Coubre, twelve miles north-west of Royan. Pathfinders dropped flares over the target; a strong north-west wind blew the flares over the town; and the air force bombed it to flinders. The Germans remained still undislodged. The French Resistance fighters brigaded into the regular French army longed to prove themselves; their local commander asked to be allowed to relieve Royan. The Free French government permitted this crime. The army bombed Royan all over again. The whole centre of the town was flattened.

Nothing, it seems to me, can atone for such folly. Yet Royan is interesting as a town built new in our day for the purpose of serving as a seaside place. It has none of the calm dignity of Brighton, our parallel city. For in the Regency it was assumed that only the upper classes would want to disport themselves in the sea. Now this *plage* is chic enough—it even has one very snobbish suburb. But it is built for families of middling people, and for motor-traffic. It is carefully, and very well, planned. The beach is lined with rich hotels. Behind them are the traffic-lanes and a market arranged so that the mother can wheel the pram, and do her shopping without going in danger of her life. Behind the market are sloping streets of pretty *châlets* for letting. The whole is charming, modern without being freakish. The most experimental thing is the church of St.-Marie. It is a very tall cement church built to suggest a ship sailing out to sea. I should hesitate to call it beautiful, and it is certainly not charming. But its interior, an upstretched space entered from half-way up, is expressive.

All this northern side of the Gironde is a series of beaches. On one occasion when I passed a day there I was reminded of *Through the Looking-Glass*:

> '*If seven maids with seven mops*
> *Swept it for half a year,*
> *Do you suppose,' the Walrus said,*
> '*That they could get it clear?'*
> '*I doubt it,' said the Carpenter,*
> *And shed a bitter tear.*

There had been a day of strong west wind. The streets of Royan were deep in sand. Huge vans equipped with vacuum machinery crawled about them sucking up the sand. I supposed that they emptied it back on to the beach.

I prefer St.-Georges-de-Didonne myself. It is a quiet *plage* a mile or two east of Royan.

By this time the traveller is fairly in the estuary of the Gironde. At Meschers the sands give place to cliffs, riddled with caves. These have sheltered a succession of inhabitants, fishers, hermits, refugee Huguenots hunted by soldiers, refugee priests hunted by republican officials, and now restaurateurs. You look down over the cliff-tops, and see the tables waiting down below. But some of the caves are simply private houses, where tourists are not welcome.

Further down the estuary is Talmont, a famous church. The tiny village crowns a rocky headland, and the church is set on the edge of the Gironde cliff. It is a Ste.-Radegonde, and is Romanesque in date. In the past its nave fell into the sea, and the rest threatened to do the same, but it has been underpinned. It is a dramatic sight, especially from the water.

Blaye is a place which one may want to see because it was the fortress of Geoffroi Rudel, the troubadour who found the castle where Richard Coeur-de-Lion was imprisoned by singing under his window; and hearing his answering song. Perhaps too, because it was the burial place of the hero Roland, where he was laid after Roncesvalles, and where his betrothed, the Belle Aude, joined him in death. But no trace of these histories remains except a few shattered walls. The Citadelle dates from the seventeenth century; the mound between the canal-port and the sea is surrounded by walls and a fosse. It is only entered by two fortified gates. The whole of the rock is tunnelled with cellars and sunken streets. A few hundred people live in these subterranean passages. The Citadelle has often been used as a prison, and it feels just like this. Its last captives were wretched victims kept there by the Gestapo during the German occupation. This may be fancy, but I have seldom felt myself in a more sinister place.

At Bourg the Gironde divides, for the tongue of land that divides the Garonne from the Dordogne lies below it. The Dordogne road runs on to Libourne, which is a far better place to spend the night than Bordeaux. A little further east is St.-Émilion, that marvellous little town, which I dare not describe here because I have done so in two other books. It is ancient, but not drowsy; on the contrary it buzzes with life, because it is the capital of the wines of the Dordogne. There is a traditional, but no longer accurate, list of the great vineyards, their names like a chime of bells along the Garonne. But in the real lists of the wine merchants St.-Émilion now nearly tops the whole. Libourne itself is frequented by importers from afar, which no doubt accounts for its comfortable inn.

4. BORDEAUX

Bordeaux is a noble city. It is also a very big one, and I shall not attempt to describe it in detail. It lies along the left bank of the Garonne, above the tidal flow, and sheltered from the west winds by the curve of the river-shore. As the traveller approaches it from the other side, it rises up in a half-moon, with the towers of the churches standing above the docks. There are two road bridges, the larger, the Pont de Pierre, leading right into the heart of the city.

Historically Bordeaux has had three great periods each marked by events of political importance. The first was under Rome. Then it was a pleasant place to live in, with gardens and schools, merchants and poets. An early barbarian invasion wrecked it, and there remains little of Roman date save some columns of the amphitheatre in the ruins of the Palais Gallien. The town revived under the Visigoths, the most civilized of the barbarians, but after the Franks from the north defeated them a decline set in and was completed by the Normans, who devastated the Garonne, and made of Bordeaux their pirates' den.

The union of rulers under the Angevins and Plantagenets restored the prosperity of the city. The Plantagenets gave it large trading privileges, and Bordeaux exported wine to England in exchange for wool. Later, as the more northerly parts of the Dukedom became involved in the conquests of the Capets, the centre of ducal power tended to shift from the north of Aquitaine to the south. Richard Coeur-de-Lion was born at Poitiers, and was called Richard de Poitiers; Richard II, the son of the Black Prince, was born in Bordeaux, and bore the name Richard of Bordeaux. Froissart records that at the later date the Gascon lords often changed their allegiance, turning from the dukes to the French kings from year to year. When the Black Prince brought Norman lords from England to command his armies in the South, they refused to treat the southern seigneurs as equals in their own country; and the Southerners were naturally alienated. The Black Prince's bosom friend the Girondin Chaptal de Buch, who commanded the right wing at the victory of Poitiers, was later captured, but remained loyal to his friend, and died miserably of neglect in the prison of the French King. But the Armagnacs of Quercy adhered to France. None the less the towns which grew rich on the trade with England were the last to lose their faith in their own dukes; and even after the French victory of Castillon, in 1453, Bordeaux organized a league of cities to rebel against the Franks. But the English armies had gone for good. The rebellion failed. The French kings abolished the privileges of the merchants, and Bordeaux, cut off from the trade with England, was ruined and went into a long period of decay.

From the last era of Aquitaine as an independent duchy date some of Bordeaux's buildings. The Cathedral was begun in the Romanesque period, though its beautiful doors and choir were made later, when the Girondin Pope Clement V reigned at Avignon. But its tower, the Pey Berland, was finished after the departure of the English, as was that of the other great Gothic church, St.-Michel. Both these tall belfries stand detached from their churches.

The third prosperous era of Bordeaux, which has lasted till the present time, began in the eighteenth century. It is responsible for the magnificent centre of the city, where whole quarters are full of stately streets and squares. Among them are the open-ended *places* built on the river, especially the famous Place des Quinconces, with Victor Louis's majestic theatre making one side of it. The royal Intendants, who liked to mark their rule by public works, built these streets; the Allées de Tourny and the

Place de Tourny remember the name of the greatest of those officials.

Bordeaux profited most from the slave-trade to the West Indies—as Bristol did in England. But nowadays it is rich principally in the wine trade, and also in forest products such as the export of resin. It breathes wealth—on the main shopping street there is one of the most impressive merchants I have ever seen: a plain shop built like a fortress of dark cement, and labelled simply with the word '*Diamants*'. The main streets are all one-way. They are terrifying to drive, and impossible to park in. Walking is also very fatiguing; but if the traveller wants to see the street-market of the Cours Victor-Hugo, which is extremely amusing, and passes the Grosse Horloge, the clock in an old gate of the city, which used to proclaim the beginning of the vintage, he must walk. No car can penetrate that close-packed crowd.

Bordeaux, it is certain, is the most notable city of the eighteenth century, next to Leningrad. The tourist, escaping from the traffic, may take one of the side streets off the centre, and suddenly find himself in silence, between plain dignified houses, in which he can imagine families of unostentatious, immensely proud people who have traded in wine for a thousand years.

It is there that I found at last a modern building to admire. The air-port is beautifully sited and proportioned.

Here is the end of the journey through Aquitaine. It began with its old capital of Bourges, in Aquitania Prima, and finishes with the capital of Aquitania Secunda, Bordeaux. Traveller, farewell.

35. Angels Adoring. Cathedral of Angoulême

36. Griffins. Aulnay

Chapter Twelve

ENVOI

―――――⟫⟪☒⟫――――――

A
t the end of the road, I have some small pieces of advice to
offer.

Advice for the road, truly. Many of the places mentioned
in this book are not upon railway lines. The roads are almost all
tarmaced, and rendered unfit for walking. This is car country,
and especially good for driving, because one can so easily get off
the main roads.

All motorists in France depend upon the Michelin road-maps.
They have two great merits: they are kept up to date, and they are
cheap. They are also large-scale, so that one is constantly falling
off one on to another. The numbers of the Michelins needed for
this book are: 63, 64, 65, 67, 68, 69, 71, 72, 73, 75.

The Michelins have defects. They are aimed exclusively at
motorists, and they do mark all roads, so that unless the driver is
really stupid he can always use them for getting from A to B.
But they do not mark contours, which is a very bad fault. Except
for a rare mention of some height on a road, and a few hatchings
to show the direction of steep slopes, they give no idea at all of
the nature of the country. When one looks at a really fine map,
such as the British Ordnance Survey or the Bartholomew or
Johnstone maps, it is easy for anybody who can map-read to
see the whole shape of the landscape. But looking at the Michelins
one cannot guess even the shape of mountains; the whole of France
might be as flat as a pancake. Contours are much more important
to the motorist than mileage, which Michelin marks with care.

Envoi

The map-makers sell an enormous number of those road-maps; they could well afford to make a proper job of them. To walkers, for instance, they are next door to useless; for they do not even mark villages which are not on a road. I myself have walked to three unmarked by Michelin; there must be many more.

On the other hand, the green Michelin guides are very good. They are arranged alphabetically, so that it is a pity they do not each include a small-scale map. Their historic introductions to each region are admirably done. Together with them the *Guides Bleus* of the Sud-Ouest and of Auvergne are very valuable for detailed travel.

Binoculars are essential for people who are interested in the rich architecture of Aquitaine. The carvings of pillars and arches of roofs cannot be discerned without the aid of glasses, and I know few sensations stronger than the rage roused by failure to see detail which your guide tells you is wonderful, but which from far below looks like a plate of macaroni.

Aquitaine is not organized for tourists, except in the *plages* and on the *routes nationales*. The hotels are mostly unpretentious, and none the worse for that. But modern laws about working hours have created problems. The hotel staffs are no longer available from dawn till midnight. So a great many hotels are now 'Bed and Breakfast' and send their guests out to restaurants for lunch and dinner. The tired traveller may sometimes find this a burden, but on the whole it works well. But the work laws create some awkward situations. Mrs. Elliot wants to have her hair washed, and what better day than Saturday? But Mr. Elliot is short of change, and he cannot change a travellers' cheque because the banks are shut on Saturday. On Monday he gets the money, but the hairdressers are shut. So the Elliots drive away from that town in a frustrated condition. Of course the remedy is simple. Ask your *hôtelier* when you arrive.

Holidays on pay, and the shorter hours of work, have wrought a revolution in France. The English term 'le weekend' is still used, but in an expanded form. The French have become highly motorized, and they are addicted to fresh air. Hundreds of thousands of them leave the towns every Friday evening, and drive to a camp or a *châlet* in the country, where the husband can fish, and the wife cook and knit for the baby. They return on Monday night. I have heard people of the older régime bewailing this national idleness, as they call it. What it necessitates for the tourist is much more forethought in reserving rooms in hotels. It has always been imperative to book ahead for Mayday, Easter, Whitsun and June 24th, but now in any weekend it is a good idea to telephone to the inn where you mean to spend the night, or to arrive early.

This choice of the French about how to spend the modern leisure seems to me deeply exciting. They do not want to use the higher standard of living they now enjoy on more money, or bigger houses. Few Frenchmen want to become very rich; of course there are exceptions, the Gouffiers of today, but they are laughed to scorn by the modern Puss in Boots. Most Frenchmen think that the ideal life is to have enough money to be comfortable, to eat good food, and to enjoy good conversation.

If I were asked to put the elements of French civilization into a list, I should begin (1) conversation, (2) food, (3) love. For men, that is. For women, love comes at the top; and for all, religion is the joker and may turn up anywhere. French education gives careful attention to teaching children the use of their beautiful language. This encourages a life-long passion for talk. Any day you can watch a party of French people round a table in a café. They are sparking with life and enjoyment; they are talking. It is true that this excellent diversion is threatened by mass communications. Radio and television are fatal to intelligent talk. I believe that they are destructive to digestion also; I refuse to eat in a restaurant where there is the *Télé*. Fastidious hotels are marked in the Michelin Red Book as 'television barred'. Radio is very poor in France anyhow, for they have chosen the worst of both worlds. The news services are controlled by the government, with the natural result that even when they are telling the truth about any political matter, nobody believes a word they say. Entertainment is commercial; it is largely trivial, banal, or vulgar.

Food next, the aspect of life that affects the traveller most of all. In Aquitaine the food is usually good, but not outstanding. You can always depend on good fish, and good bread and cheese. Wine is too high and solemn a subject for me to write about it. I trustfully ask the host to give me a local wine, almost always with satisfactory results. For instance I was given almost the best red wine of my life at Loudun. Of course as you approach the south you are in the country of the great wines of Bordeaux, and it is part of the experience of French travel to drink one of the famous vintages sometimes.

France has reversed the mediaeval list of the Seven Deadly Sins, in one case at least. Greed is no longer a Deadly Sin, but a Cardinal Virtue. France puts eating in its proper place, and that is at the top of civilized occupations. It is not necessarily best at its most dear. I mistrust dolled-up restaurants, especially those which have bogus antique decorations and call themselves '*Auberges*'. I will tell here a tale of Poitiers.

I had tried a hotel recommended by a guidebook and found the rooms poor and the food uneatable. They served meat hard from the refrigerator; and moreover played a base though common trick by offering as *table d'hôte* a meal so nasty that their guests were forced to order much dearer items off the *à la carte* menu. I found a charming bed-and-breakfast hotel, but wanted impartial advice on restaurants. As I was changing money at the Crédit Lyonnais bank, I asked the woman cashier if she could recommend me a restaurant where I could eat modestly and decently. She blushed and said that she lived at home and did not know restaurants, but she would ask a colleague. He collected another, and in three minutes the entire exchange department of the Crédit Lyonnais was gathered in a passionate discussion. Then the senior, a most impressive person, came forward and said: 'Mademoiselle, we think you should try the Plat d'Étain. It is small and quiet and clean, and one eats well there.' They were as clever as bankers ought to be; for the Plat d'Étain suited my tastes exactly. I used it on my many visits to Poitiers. But dearly as I like them, I simply cannot imagine myself asking the staff of the Bank of Scotland in Edinburgh to tell me where to go for good food.

Women will say, 'What about Love?' France is now undergoing her second period of romantic love. The first was the Age of Romance, whose capital was Aquitaine. Marriage then was, of course, a matter of arrangement, of property and inheritance. Yet love came bursting in. So the troubadours sang of love, almost always between a lady and a lover not her husband. For a woman possessed of a dowry would probably not have seen her husband till her betrothal, and it was pure luck if she grew to love him, whereas handsome bachelors were likely to turn up at the castle, and to fall in love. The romantic era of song was crushed by the conquests of the Frankish North. Its successor was the age of the Celtic romances, the tales of Arthur and of Tristram, and of sentiment such as that of the Romaunt of the Rose. But in life, till half a century ago, marriage in the bourgeois and upper classes was a matter for arrangement. This found a natural compensation in the strength of family relations. A woman might never grow to love her husband, but she adored her son. This family feeling is reflected in French law, where the family is protected in every way. It embodies something like the Roman *patria potestas*. A father may no longer imprison his son for disobedience, as he could before the Revolution. But it is still very difficult to rescue children from cruel parents.

Modern education and sports have greatly narrowed the gap between young men and women. You cannot conveniently take a chaperon up a mountain to ski, or into a university lecture to watch the studenst looking at each other rather than at the professor. My memory goes back to the days when segregation began to disintegrate. I believe that the modern state of social relations is far happier. It may be dangerous—though relations always were dangerous—but it is at least natural.

France remains entirely herself, no matter how manners alter, and that is why travel in France is an adventure. The British traveller having crossed the narrow strait of the Channel, finds himself further abroad than if he had crossed the Atlantic. He notices instantly the outward signs of *la Civilisation française*, a mode of manners and customs taught uniformly to every French child.Soon he realizes that this surface culture does not in the least impede an individualism so strong that it frees every man and woman from the need to conform to the minds of his neighbours. Almost the only common feature of the French is their intensity, so that whatever they are doing, they do it with all their might. The French are interesting as people. This is why one cannot travel in France without hearing and being astonished by strange tales of history. To me, they are irresistibly lovable, so that to wander among them gives me delight.

'*Adieu, bon voyage*', say the French. 'Goodbye, good journey.' The poets say all things about feeling better than others. Let Walter de la Mare say for me what I have received from France:

> *Look thy last on all things lovely,*
> *Every hour. Let no night*
> *Seal thy sense in deathly slumber*
> *Till to delight*
> *Thou have paid thy utmost blessing;*
> *Since that all things thou wouldst praise*
> *Beauty took from those who loved them*
> *In other days.*

Appendix One

ACKNOWLEDGEMENTS

I owe deep gratitude to the Centre d'Etudes Supérieures de Civilisation Médiévale of Poitiers. Its Director, Monsieur le Professeur René Crozet, and his assistants Mademoiselle Ouvrard and Monsieur Henri Renou, gave me a kind welcome, helped me to use their wonderful library of photographs, and told me how to find places which, without their advice, I should not have seen.

I wish to thank Artaud Frères of Nantes for permission to reproduce their photograph of La Rochelle and Monsieur A. Gilbert of Jarnac for permission to reproduce his photograph of the façade of the cathedral at Angoulême. I am grateful, also, to Monsieur Bernard Biraben of Bordeaux for permission to reproduce photographs of St.-Savin, of the Lanterne des Morts of Château Larcher, the Lion of St.-Amand-de-Boixe, the Griffins of Aulnay, the church of Ste.-Marie-la-Grande of Poitiers, St.-Savin, the Hosanna Cross, and the Cavalier of Parthenay. The Archives Nationales Photographiques have kindly allowed me to reproduce the royal tombs of Fontrevault, a pillar-capital of St.-Pierre-de-Chauvigny, and the tower of le Dorat. For all those who showed me kindness in France, I wish that some day they may receive the courtesy from another that once they gave to a foreigner in their own land.

My acknowledgement is due to the Literary Trustees of Walter de la Mare and The Society of Authors as their representative for permission to quote the last stanza of his poem 'Fare Well', from *Collected Poems*.

167

Appendix Two

HOTELS

The hotels listed here are some that I have stayed in. They represent only a few, in a country where every town and most villages have inns. My own tastes are marked. I like small hotels, kept by a family. I do not like 'Luxury' hotels. To my mind, quietude is even more necessary than good food, though food is often, in Aquitaine, very good. Hotels which I have found specially good are marked with a X. Hotels without a restaurant are marked B. (Bed and Breakfast).

Place	*Department*	*Hotel*
Aigre	Charente	France (X)
Angoulême	Charente	Palais (X)
Aubusson	Creuse	France
Bourges	Cher	Boule d'Or (X)
Châteauneuf-sur-Charente	Charente	Trois Piliers
Châtellerault	Vienne	Grand Hôtel Moderne
Chatenet-en-Dognon (Pont-du-Dognon)	Haute Vienne	Châlet du Lac (X)
Coulon	Deux-Sèvres	Centrale
Gargilesse	Indre	Artistes
Glenic	Creuse	Moulin-Noyé
Gueret	Creuse	Au Clair (X)
Libourne	Gironde	Loubat (X)
Limoges	Haute Vienne	Grand Hôtel Moderne
Loudun	Vienne	Roue d'Or
Melle	Deux-Sèvres	Centrale
Montluçon	Allier	Terminus

Montmorillon	Vienne	France
Niort	Deux-Sèvres	Grand Hôtel Sadoun
Parthenay	Deux Sèvres	Grand Hôtel Birot
Poitiers	Vienne	Europe (BX)
La Rochelle	Charente-Maritime	Commerce (X)
Les Roches Prémarie	Vienne	Clos des Roches
Saintes	Charente-Maritime	Commerce (X)
Thouars	Deux-Sèvres	Cheval Blanc

Appendix Three

BIBLIOGRAPHY

I. GUIDEBOOKS

The standard guidebooks to France are the *Guides Bleus* (pub. Hachette.) Those concerned with the region of this book are:

Auvergne
Sud-Ouest
Poitou et Guyenne.
Michelin guidebooks.

France: the 'red Michelin'. This guide is indispensable as a guide to restaurants and hotels. Its recommendations are based almost entirely upon food. It is not inclusive, there are many good inns not listed in Michelin.

Green Guides. Those regional Michelin guides are excellent. They give a geological introduction, and then places of interest in alphabetical order. They also give directions for tours; these are long, and do not allow for the tourist's desire to look at places in detail.

Both the red and the green Michelins have town-plans. *Logis de France* (pub. La Fédération nationale des Logis de France, 21 Rue d'Artois, Paris 8). This gives more inclusive lists than Michelin, and is invaluable for the more simple hotels and lodgings.

Syndicats d'Initiative. Almost all towns and many villages have *syndicats d'initiative*. These are information offices, which will give the tourist local lists of hotels and places of interest. They also give away brochures, often very well done, of local tours.

2. BOOKS

It is difficult to recommend books about the provinces of France. French historians pay little attention to anywhere but what they call 'the seat of Power'; that is, Paris. There is one old book which gives a vivid impression of Aquitaine in the Middle Ages: Froissart's *Chronicles of England, France and Spain*. The series Horizon de France (Hachette) have recently re-published regional books. *Poitou* is excellent; *Limousin* useful. The books contain articles by experts on geography, history, art, etc. and are admirably illustrated.

INDEX

Index

Index

Index